# Unseen

# Unseen

*Intersecting Faith & Sexuality in the Bible Belt*

WRITTEN BY MEREDITH JADE

# ACKNOWLEDGEMENTS

To my sister, for being my rock—and the first to read and affirm my words.

To Kelsey, for being my cheerleader and wellspring of positivity.

To Brandi, for being a kindred spirit and crusader.

To Claire, for helping me see the mistakes I didn't.

To Alissa, for giving me the constructive critique I needed.

To Susan, for that long phone call preparing me for this process.

To Brittany, for examining the text for gentleness and guiding me with the Gospel.

*For my wife.*

# FOREWORD
## BY SUSAN COTTRELL

To navigate into adulthood, whole and healed from life's wounds, is a challenge for anyone. But to discover that *your parents AND GOD stand against who you are at the deepest core*—well, that rocks your entire life.

When my own daughters came out as queer, I had to look anew at everything from our twenty-five years in the evangelical church. I rethought many beliefs, *but loving and embracing my children was not one of them.*

It was our family's story that pulled me into the sharp divide between the evangelical church and gay Christians. But it was stories like Meredith's that thrust me into full time advocacy. These families were crying out for help.

I have worked with countless gay Christians who must choose between their family's love and who they *know* themselves to be. Or as Meredith writes, "gay Christians who are caught in a dark and lonely space of having to choose spirituality or emotional authenticity." My epiphany with my two daughters is that *our spirituality is consistent with our emotional authenticity!*

Every day, families and churches are throwing out people like Meredith, "sheep who've been pushed astray... forced to [choose between] God or Love." That is a choice *no one* should ever have to make.

Meredith tells her story so beautifully, so authentically, you will be pulled along in its current, rising and falling with each turn. I shoved aside a pile of work to read her book, unable to put it down! I laughed, grieved, and cheered for Meredith all along the way.

Get a nice, hot drink, sit back in a comfy chair, and enjoy this book. It is for gay Christians, their parents, and the church that aspires to love like Jesus. It is a story we all need to know.

Love,
Susan Cottrell
FreedHearts

# INTRODUCTION

*I thought she went to church* was the first rumor I heard upon returning to work the week after I came out. After undergoing the persecution of telling my family, posting our relationship on social media was a heartening distraction. Hundreds of beautiful comments bolstered the fragile confidence I held, but it only took one nasty remark to undo it all. As my heart sank, my indignation rose and they collided in a fiery mess in the middle of my gut. My mind was suddenly overcome with reasons why I should retaliate and justify what I felt. I wanted to rush home and write a series of blogs that would deflect any naysayers. As much as I appreciated those who congratulated me saying, "Be yourself and don't care what other people think," the sentiment was not at all comforting. The thought of irrational statements and opinions about me whirling about without my knowledge irked me to the very core. I wanted to have a mature, theological debate while simultaneously stomping my feet and crying that it just wasn't fair. But what was fair to me? Did fairness imply equality or was it merited based on my reasoning as opposed to someone else's? The complexities of the different definitions of "fair" brought me to a simple conclusion: that I wasn't the judge of what was fair, thus I did not have to announce to the world my rationale for loving a girl.

The pages hereafter are a culmination of every emotion I held at bay, every text I wanted to send, every post I wanted to share and every retaliation left unsaid. These words are tear-stained, and my only petition, page after page, was that my patience be rewarded. The day I relinquished the fact that I couldn't change people's opinion about me was the day I truly began to feel at peace. For months, I girded myself with theological defenses, ready at a moment's notice to combat skepticism with my own progressive Biblical beliefs. As polished as my cultural and clerical references were, I continued to hit a fundamental wall. But then that's when I realized it. I realized that no person could ever know how I felt unless they, too, were gay and Christian. They couldn't feel the ache of dread at the thought of creating a fake and listless heterosexual family. They couldn't feel the warmth of assurance I felt when I met the love of my life, nor could they feel the beautiful fear of when I accepted that truth. They hadn't met the near-flawless, most purely altruistic person I have ever met or loved. That's why I stopped trying to justify myself.

At the end of the day, after I'd read all the critical articles I could, and after I'd exhausted myself with searching for redemption, I only had to look into Allison's eyes to truly know. My mom used to tell me that I had the best discernment of anyone she knew. I would screen television shows for my sister, be an ethical voice of reason in my peer group, and react to those spiritual gut-feelings I couldn't explain. I felt that similar guidance when I looked at Allison, and I've never been so certain about someone's character. Even if I didn't believe a word of theology, was skeptical of my own morality, and doubted every truth within myself, all of that would be wiped away because of the trust I have in my soulmate. Never have I met someone so grounded, compassionate, and real. Unfortunately some people will never see past the gender to see the person. And I ache for those who will never understand or even stop to consider.

These pages are for the "oxymoron outcasts," the gay Christians who are caught in a dark and lonely space of having to choose spirituality or emotional authenticity. These pages are for the allies who want to congratulate me for more than just "being myself," but for crying out on behalf of God's unconditional love. These pages are for the sheep who've been pushed astray because of the hatred people spew at your "choice," when the only choice you've been forced to make is God *or* Love. These pages are for the people who will forever be in disagreement. I respect your conviction but challenge you to see how I feel. Our opinions aren't gospel. Even mine.

# 1

## JUST AS I AM

"Take your hymnals and turn to page 307," the music minister said as the organ began to hum. "We'll sing the first, second, and last verses."

The old, familiar tune rang out, and the minister's arms began to sway in rhythm with the lines of *Just As I Am*. The song was a Southern Baptist staple, and one that had taken up permanent residence on the invitational line of every Sunday's bulletin. Too bad the title's concept wasn't taken as seriously as the routine of singing it.

I wondered why we never used any other hymns besides that one. I also wondered why verses three through six were always neglected. If allowed to make my own selection, I would've chosen my favorite hymn, *Turn Your Eyes Upon Jesus*. There were random, out-of-tune pianos in abandoned Sunday school rooms throughout the church with dusty hymnals in their benches, and I'd sometimes sneak away to play the enchanting melody. I don't know why I gravitated toward the simple, soothing message of "Oh soul, are you weary and troubled." What would a nine-year-old know of weariness?

"Verse three," redirected the minister, and his arms continued to wave in a hypnotic manner. The altar would have to be full and the invitation prolonged before the other verses got their chance. The tenor voice of the minister, pronounced through pulpit microphone, drowned the small murmurs of the choir as he sang.

"Listen to the message. He is bidding, asking, begging us to respond. Come down to the front and make that decision today," the preacher said, like he was pitching an infomercial product that only had moments remaining until the three *easy payments* offer was off the table. "What would happen if you walked out of these church doors today and got hit by a bus without having first repented and surrendered your life?"

As he paced around the front steps of the altar, wiping his brow with a handkerchief, admonishing his flock, and waiting, I was suddenly hyper-aware of a lurking feeling in my stomach. Although I couldn't understand the ramifications at the time, my body, in that moment of the invitation, felt suffocated by a blanket of anxiety that seemed to be descending on the congregation like a great, invisible fog. My worrisome heart struggled beneath it, fighting for air. Craning my neck to the side, I looked at my dad's wrist watch, hoping the hands were aligned at noon.

"That sensation you feel inside right now is conviction," said my pastor, as if he sensed my fear. "Don't deny it. Don't let Satan steal that conviction and keep you from coming forward. That still, small voice is the Holy Spirit telling you to make a decision today. Don't delay; don't let the devil whisper and tempt you otherwise. Let the Lord lead, guide, and direct you." Words "lead," "guide," and "direct" used in succession were iconic Baptist turns-of-phrase.

Uncertainty crept over me like a cold shadow, and I held tight to my daddy's hand. What was I feeling? I had gone to the front to make an outward profession of my faith several years back. I had been baptized in the waters behind the choir loft. I had even rededicated my life at Bible school the previous summer. It was like continuously renewing a library book that I already owned. Granted, there was an actual date when I took my mom's hand and walked down the aisle to tell my congregation that I was a Christian, but having grown up in church and with a devout family, I was constantly immersed. I hadn't made a decision, per se. I had been receptive to teachings, sensitive to the Holy Spirit, and a lover of Jesus's stories my whole life. Why now, long after I'd made it public, did I fear that "still, small voice?" It haunted me. Did my salvation have an expiration date? I felt compelled to run down the aisle, and I envisioned the devil nipping at my heels all the way.

Worry wasn't new. I dealt with it often. Many nights when I was younger, I had woken up, sweaty and confused, and run down the hallway to my parents' room. I'd crept past the threshold and peeked over their bed to make sure their bodies were still there, rising and falling with slow

breaths. Looking back, it was as if roles were reversed—
a child checking on her sleeping parents. Sometimes
when the house fell quiet, I'd wonder if the rapture had
occurred and left me behind, sinful and alone. My most
paralyzing nightmare was finding only my parents' clothing lying in a pile on the floor. When I invariably found
them safe in their beds, I was relieved beyond belief, reassured that I'd not sinned too much as to make me exempt
from a wonderful eternity in heaven with them. When my
little sister came along and was sleeping in the twin bed
beside me, I didn't have to make the trek down the hallway. Rebekah was still under that age-of-accountability
umbrella the preacher talked about—the age window in
which we were still promised heaven no matter what. The
older I got, the more I felt my own "blessed assurance"
slipping away.

The finality of death and fear of missing eternity woke
me from dreamless sleeping on many occasions. Worst-
case scenarios and tragedies played out in my head like
movie trailers, dominating my thoughts with possibilities
of how life would come to an end, or how the end of others'
lives would leave me alone. Sermon after sermon warned
me of such impending death, the "what ifs," and lists of
unforgivables. What if I and the people I loved were doing these things unknowingly? Awaiting sentencing at the
gates of heaven was my biggest fear, and at nine years old,
I lived each day wondering what I was doing that would
send me straight to hell. Somehow I missed the beautiful
part about grace and love.

The last chords of the invitational hymn died away, and stragglers at the altar returned to their seats. When I realized that no one had gone down to get saved, be baptized, rededicate, join the church, or give their testimony, I felt an odd mixture of pity and fear. Would our preacher leave if he didn't reach his soul commission or Sunday School attendance goal? He had preached his heart out. He had yelled until his faced turned red and the decibel readings on his microphone matched the hue of his fiery temples. Daddy and I sat behind the soundboard in the balcony, and I would sometimes count the number of times the sound guy would adjust the mic volume. After such a loud and fiery evangelical message, I thought that surely someone would be seated in the front row filling out their decision card. Instead, impatient congregation members were sneaking from their pews so they could beat the Methodists to lunch.

# 2

## GIRL POWER

I jumped out of the car and ran inside the only convenience store between my house and the soccer field that sold the kind of Gatorade I liked. It wasn't just the flavor— it was the twist top. I loved having the twist-top drinks that I could squirt in my mouth like football players did on the sidelines. Whatever I could do to be "one of the boys," I did.

"I like your shirt," the store clerk said as she took my dollar and change.

I beamed and said, "Thanks!"

Rummaging through my t-shirt drawer was a customary ritual on Tuesdays and Thursdays. These days were soccer practice days. They were days I religiously watched the Doppler radar and prayed practice wouldn't be rained out. They were days I wanted nothing more than for my favorite shirt to be clean. Seldom shopping in the girls' department, I was amused to finally find a "girly" shirt which accurately represented my sentiments toward sports and frankly, my competitive nature in general. Clad in a bright turquoise shirt with a soccer ball and the slogan, "Girls rule, boys drool," I marched to the car, fancy sports drink in hand. I never knew if my fellow teammates cared about my t-shirt mantra, but I would sprint onto that freshly mown sanctuary and wear my declaration proudly. Coed soccer teams were the bane of my adolescent existence. Boys acted like the girls were invisible on the field, and boy did that fire me up. I was a pretty great little player, or so my mom said. I was thankful she sat in her fold-up chair on the sidelines during practice to commiserate with me — and to take out my earrings before games. I couldn't do that myself.

The sentiment of my t-shirt manifested during those U10 soccer days in an honest desire to not only be one of the boys but to *outshine* the boys. This also became a telling and common theme in my relationship with them as I got older. Whereas most straight girls contended for *attention* from boys, I was contending *with* them in an attempt to emulate them. I was like an under-cover apprentice of sorts. Their clothes were much cooler, and I wanted to be strong like them. As a kid, I had no idea that these subconscious ambitions would later evolve into wanting the love boys had, too. Being the emotional adolescent I was, I just saw boys as the enemy always stealing all my best friends— but damn, I wanted to be just like them anyway.

There was one practice in particular which I remember distinctly. I'd been so lucky as to be captain of a scrimmage team and chosen to play forward, my favorite position. Although my coach didn't keep score (a custom I thought to be absurd), the tally was indeed kept in my head. Near the end of practice, when dusk was beginning to sneak on the field and depth perception was beginning to become skewed, I got a chance to go for a penalty kick. It was my time to shine. The opposing goalie was a snarky little boy, and I was taking the stage to dethrone him from his lofty pedestal. My team cheered me on as I gazed at the net and formulated a strategy. The goalie would be expecting trickery and looked prepared to dive, so I thought I'd keep it simple. Just as I stepped back to make the goal of my dreams, the coach blew his whistle.

"Wait a second," he said as he waddled toward me. He was a hefty fellow to be a soccer coach. "Let's make this interesting. All you guys, get in the goal. She's a good shot, so let's make her work for it!"

I knew it was all in jest. For God's sake, it was the end of a Tuesday night scrimmage game for a U10 recreation league, not the World Cup. But it was *my* World Cup. Being an advocate for all the girls on that field who had been made fun of or trampled was *my* figurative goal for *my* team and one that was about to be taken away from me. Granted, this all sounds very dramatic for an otherwise even-tempered kid, but I felt programmed with a special duty, and it all started with making that goal.

All the boys lined the net from post to post. There was not a real feasible way to get it through them because they were practically linking arms. My only hope was getting it over the boys' heads and past their leaping reach without completely overshooting, which was an embarrassment in its own right. I stood, poised. Taking three steps back and breathing in slowly, I envisioned my laces scooping the ball and placing it exactly where I wanted it. The kick felt right as soon as it left my foot. Sailing directly above the frantic hands and precisely beneath the crossbar, the ball grazed the post with such finesse that it ricocheted at a sharp angle toward the back of the net. None of the dozen hands even had a chance. I nearly kicked up my heels with delight. The girls cheered, and the boys in the goal dispersed, acting if it they were suddenly disinterested in such child's play. The glory only lasted for a few seconds, but it was euphoric.

# 3

## FICTIONAL

My favorite place to be as a child, besides the soccer field, was Mamaw's house—a magical place of VHS sing-along movies, playing pretend, and all the special snacks I didn't often get at home. Before Mom quit work and we started homeschooling, I would go there in the afternoons. I couldn't wait to see her car in the pickup line at school. While I labored over the rows and rows of videos, Mamaw would heat my toaster pastry. She would wait patiently as I made icing designs on my snack, being sure to squeeze every drop from the corners of the packet. I was required to sit at the table, though, so none of the blueberry filling would ooze onto the carpet.

Disney movies were always my first choice. I loved any of the iconic 90s classics, although I was never as much a fan of the princess stories as I was of the more adventurous or animal-themed ones. My favorites were *Aladdin* and *The Lion King*, featuring the best Disney soundtrack of all time. My Elton John fandom apparently began young. I mostly watched movies so I could reenact them, and let's be honest, being the fearless hero didn't mean playing the part of Snow White. Granted, Disney has done a lot better lately at making strong, female characters whose aim is more than securing a prince, but back in the 90s, I had to play the boy role if I wanted to have any fun. And the injustice of only having princess underwear to choose from! What was the crime in Ninja Turtles and Scooby-Doo for girls?

This mindset stuck with me through adolescence and into my adulthood. Admittedly my protests weren't regarding animated characters at this point, but rather in how I viewed the people in my life. I saw people based on their traits, talent, and quirks and was drawn to those things, craving only to bask in those I loved and admired. My mindset of love stayed pure well into my 20s, mainly because I was painfully shy, naive, and modest regarding anything that veered romantic or sexual. I was frightened to no end by the very idea of ever loving or finding love powerful enough to finally take such a step. Not until recently was I able to qualify this aspect of myself as something unique and intrinsic to the way I loved—loyally and fervently, no matter what. The problem was that I'd yet to find someone to love me as fervently *back*, though I was vaguely aware that that's what falling in love might one day feel like—being so ardently drawn to someone, and them reciprocating a feeling so powerful that it makes you doubt you could ever love enough to keep up.

Until the day I was to find that type of love, I saturated myself with characters I adored. Turns out Jo March, Idgie Threadgood, Anne of Green Gables, and even Elphaba, all had one thing in common. They were not only women I admired; they were women I loved, and they each were the type of woman to love me back.

# 4

# PILLAR OF SALT

One Monday afternoon when I was fifteen years old, I took a break from my school work to watch the season premiere of a new talkshow. Together, my mom and I watched the first (hilarious) monologue of what would soon become a smash hit daytime talkshow. There was no guessing about Ellen. She was openly gay and a spokesperson for the LGBT community, but she didn't parade her sexuality on the show as if her life revolved around it. The show wasn't about indoctrinating activism or displaying bitterness toward non-supporters, but rather about creating a space where everyone, regardless of their opinion, could come to laugh.

As we watched Ellen begin her new comedic journey, my mom sighed and said, "I love her, but what a waste."

I was silent, nodding my head in compliant agreement, wondering what that could possibly mean. Was my mom upset that Ellen's humor could not be traditionally passed on in a heterosexual relationship? Was she saying that Ellen was only authenticated by a man? Did she mean that Ellen was destined for hell for loving a woman? Or did she mean that her extravagant efforts to spread a message of love and togetherness was useless because *some* of society deemed her abnormal? None of the answers would have been good ones, so I let it go and continued to nod. Because the flickering question in the back of my head was, "Would she be upset if I loved a girl too?"

The conversation piqued my interest in this poor woman deemed to be a waste, so I decided to do a little research. I mainly associated Ellen with an innocent and forgetful blue fish, and I wanted to know more. It was the latter end of my middle school years, and my family shared one laptop that was anchored to an internet router in my parents' room. I flipped open the old machine one afternoon and listened to the whir of the fan while I connected to the internet. I read about Ellen's stand-up career and saw that she had her own sitcom, on which she actually came out publicly. There were heartfelt Oprah interviews, seemingly foreshadowing Ellen's impending success in the talkshow world, and endless videos of her comedy routines. Her personality was contagious and her delivery impeccable. Ellen was a fascinating person.

Then I began to feel frightened. Why did Ellen make me feel safe? Why did I admire her so much? I accused myself of being swindled into a sinful mindset, and I suddenly viewed myself with unrelenting disparagement. I hated myself. I closed every page, wiped the internet history, and worried about my salvation. Even clearing the computer's history was probably deceptive. I fought tears, wondering why I was such a disappointment. I was a good kid. Good kids weren't supposed to disappoint their parents.

I ran to my room and flipped through the pages of my little pink Bible until I reached that iconic and loathsome story in the Old Testament, Sodom and Gomorrah. As if figuratively whipping myself into submission, I read the underlined passage. In childlike pen was written a date and the name of an old Baptist pastor who had been at my church years ago, and etched into the margins, in all caps, was the statement: homosexuality is a sin.

Even though I tried to be the best child in the world for my parents, I was awful and disobedient. I grabbed a pen, and with hurried precision, scratched out the words. The thin paper ripped. I wept bitter, confused tears and collapsed on my bed like a pillar of salt.

# 5

## SOMETHING MISSING

When I was in college, I was practically as incorrupt as that middle schooler watching Ellen stand-up on slow internet. I had never been drunk, never missed my 10 p.m. curfew, was never tweaked out on any drug (unless antihistamine grogginess counted). I didn't cuss, had never been kissed, had never even gotten a speeding ticket. Throw in the fact that I had been homeschooled, and my life was perhaps more chaste than the average kindergartener. My life essentially consisted of commuting to class, coming home to bury myself in homework, and going to church three times a week. I loved those things. They weren't chores, really.

One could argue over what percentage of my compliant behavior was due to nature as opposed to nurture, but I found it to be a complementary (albeit consuming) combination. I was naturally inclined to be a servant, cautious and aloof in most social situations. I loved seeing people happy, and when they weren't, I took on the task of trying to fix the problem. In our extremely conservative and traditional home, my aversion to worldly and communal things was a perfect match for my family's expectations, especially my mom's. I was never "good" under protest, and I never rebelled. I simply stayed home because it made both me *and* my family happy.

To this day, I have an aversion to sounds that imply anger and non-compliance. Slamming doors, stomping, and loud voices make me cringe. While I lived at home, my bedroom door was usually open unless I was changing clothes. If I ever *did* close it, though, I would carefully twist the handle until the lever latch was inside the door and close it silently before allowing the latch release into the doorframe. When we took up the carpeting in the hallway and replaced it with hardwood, I walked on the balls of my feet so as not to make what I thought to be "frustrated walking sounds."

Regardless of how I longed to mask them, I experienced my share of frustrations. With each new experience, worldly defilement exposed me to a realm I was not yet ready to experience. All of my dating experiences, though sparse, lacked that joyful connection, that spark. Each one taught me only things I *didn't* want. I continued to be failed by emotions I could not seem to muster. Problem being, I was trying to fill a shell of a human with a checklist of traits instead of looking for the person.

During my last semester of college, my eyes latched on to a boy in the music department who seemed to be everything I wanted. His porcelain skin, skinny jeans, styled hair, and guitar player groove had me superficially smitten. I was always drawn to effeminate qualities. I knew him vicariously through a friend and kept up with his dating life. I went to some of his shows and hung out in some of the same places, basically just making my presence known until further notice. After a few weeks, I heard that he was newly single, and we started talking. I went to some of his band's shows, we hung out after class, and we went together to get our first tattoos. If that isn't potential love, I don't know what is. One evening after we had been seeing each other casually for a while, he invited me over to his house in a neighborhood close to campus. It seemed innocent enough.

Stepping into his room was like tripping and falling into a Lewis Carroll book. The black-lit room glistened with psychedelic colors, his pet iguana (equally as colorful) sat quizzically in a cage, and lava lamps bubbled upward in vibrant blobs. The cramped room had only a small space to walk through, while the rest was occupied by a bed and pristinely organized electric pianos, sound boards, and other music paraphernalia.

He sifted through his movie collection while I was in the bathroom. I applied some chapstick and dwelled on an embarrassing blemish for too long, then stood there looking at myself in the mirror, wondering if I was desirable enough. I was so tired of the emotional burden of having never been kissed. After a decoy flush of the toilet and a final, silent pep-talk, I emerged.

A movie was playing, and he was propped up on some pillows. I followed suit, feeling excited and terrified all at the same time. Within minutes, he lurked closer, staring at me with predatory eyes. He then hovered over me, his black clothing and the shadows making him seem more like a menacing storm than anything romantic. I laid there motionless as he rubbed himself over me, teasing me with kisses on my cheek and wisps of his groping hand. Why was I feeling more violated than excited? Making his way toward my face, he kissed me gently. I didn't exactly kiss back because I didn't know how. Instead, I sat back, feeling somehow lighter as that never-been-kissed burden finally lifted.

Before I knew it, my first kiss grabbed a belt from his bedside table and began strapping my arms to the headboard. My heart raced. *This is what you wanted*, I told myself. *This is what people do. You should like this.* He did nothing more than restrain me, explore me with his hands, and then proceed to tell me all his sadomasochistic fantasies. Although still traumatic, I was not violated in any way other than emotionally. When he discovered I was not a willing candidate and that my body was not how he liked it, I was released and left sitting there feeling like an inanimate object. All I wanted to do was go home.

"That was my first kiss," I awkwardly blurted out. I don't know why I felt compelled to reveal such private information. Maybe it was to justify my hesitance and discomfort with the whole situation. Maybe it was to make him feel bad for ruining my first semblance of intimacy.

"Had I known that, I would've made it a lot better," he admitted egotistically. He seemed suddenly ashamed, and I was glad of it. He should have been.

After a silent exchange of obligatory hugs, I exited quickly and walked to my car. I left his house that night feeling defiled and embarrassed, a film of confused disgust veiling my mind and body like a gross pollutant.

That shroud of discomfort followed me for the next two years. It walked with me on stage to receive my diploma; it seeped into my belongings and travelled with me to a new city after graduation; it shifted my gaze away from any potential love interest; and it whispered to me daily that I would never again be willing to be vulnerable. From then on, I attributed my aversion to men to my shitty first experience, never considering that I might not have wanted anything resembling such an experience.

As months passed, I acclimated to a new city, a new job, new friends, and new adventures. It was weird being away from home, not having a curfew, and buying my own groceries. Figuring out my life helped me to forget the invisible bondage I'd once felt regarding my dating life— or lack thereof. Maybe I was ready to get out there and try again. Then again, maybe I was just ready to shed my "never been in an official relationship" status. I was self-conscious of my inexperience and mortified that I was basically disinterested when it came to meeting guys. *I* didn't even understand it, so I definitely didn't feel equipped to answer questions about dating and relationships, talk about my nonexistent sex life, or God forbid, go to a penis-themed bachelorette party. That was my nightmare. I was in a rut, but I couldn't decide if climbing out of that rut was really my desire or if it was just because I was expected to.

I was working at a daycare when I met Jason. His three-year-old daughter, Ella, was in my classroom, and she was admittedly my favorite. Her quirky behavior, lanky limbs, and huge eyes were beyond endearing. Being mid-morning staff, I didn't come into contact with the parents unless they came to retrieve their little ones early. I met Jason on one such day. When he walked in, Ella was in my lap working on a coloring sheet. I caught his eye, saw his thin frame and knew she belonged to him. Jumping up to get her things, I met him at the door with a clipboard so he could sign her out. As I leaned discreetly over to see his name on the page, I could smell the same clean detergent scent that was on Ella's beloved blanket. I'm not sure if the scent alone was intoxicating or if it was simply the notion of my interest in him. We exchanged dad and daycare employee niceties, and they went on their way.

"He's going through a terrible divorce," my coworker said, as if she could see the transcript of my investigative mind.

"Oh?" I wasn't sure if she was deterring me, giving me the green-light to pursue him, or simply feeding me a fact, but I felt a sudden and crippling wave of pity. "How sad. That's so, so sad."

During subsequent weeks, I waited and wondered when Jason would come back. I didn't know what I'd do if I *did* see him, but the anticipation of it all kept afloat my hopes that my ability to be attracted to someone had not withered away. One day, when I had almost forgotten that I was waiting to see him, Jason came to pick up Ella.

I quickly volunteered to sign her out, nearly tripping over a plastic xylophone in the process. I met him at the door. He looked tired as he signed and picked up his little girl.

"It has been a stressful morning," he sighed. "Been dealing with custody disputes."

"I'm so sorry," I replied, at a loss for what else to say. As I rummaged around my brain for any other hopeful statement, they left.

That afternoon, I stealthily stalked Jason on social media and sent him a short but encouraging message. When his reply was immediate, I was actually excited. What an uncommon feeling. Would I finally be able to shake the apprehension that had followed me since my first kiss? My heart felt revived and brisk, bravely denying any doubts I might have. Jason and I hit it off quickly. He owned a paintball facility and was a calm and authentic guy. I had no complaints. We had even kissed a few times, and I was still hanging around. And there were gleeful times after a fun date when I thought I would be with him forever.

Then there were times when I felt listless, disinterested, and slightly grossed out by the way his lips felt when he kissed me. Pretty soon, the latter sentiment began to overtake the joyous ones, and I felt myself spiraling downward into a guilty chasm. What I had mistaken for affection was actually pity for Jason's situation, and the moment I realized that, I was clambering to get away. I became non-responsive, callous, and nearly avoidant. I started going to parties and dance clubs on the weekends instead of hanging out with Jason. Drowning myself in cheap beer and loud rap music created a blur that helped me forget I was interested in him—or any guy for that matter.

The collision of disinterest in Jason, the vulnerability, and the blur removed my inhibitions and made me brave. I confidently ignored Jason's repeated requests to hang out, replacing him with female friends I adored. They made me forget. During all this mess, I ended up kissing a girl— the same girl on several occasions, actually. I hated myself for doing it, and for enjoying it, and blamed the alcohol for my impaired judgement. Reassuring myself that it was just a "stage," I fell asleep each night praying for forgiveness and to be suddenly and irrevocably in love with Jason. But I soon realized that no amount of self-inflicted pressure or prayer could make me feel anything for him other than pity— pity that he'd been treated so cruelly by his ex-wife, and now by me.

Jason knew something was going on. We met one last time at a sushi restaurant in town. We both knew it was an unspoken parting of ways, but it wasn't until the check came that either of us had the guts to address it.

"So what's going on?" He asked sheepishly. "Is this over?"

"I'm just not ready," I lied.

I was so ready for a relationship, but I couldn't interpret my sudden distaste for him as anything other than my own wretched indecision. Jason's eyes welled up with tears, and they began spilling over onto the receipt as he tallied the tip and signed. I was mortified that I had made a grown man cry. He then began nervously digging into his pockets, finally pulling out a skeleton key that he placed on the table.

"Happy early birthday," he said as he got up. "It has your initials engraved on it, so it's yours. Keep it."

I took the key in my hands and tilted it so that the light reflected off the grooved lettering. Old skeleton keys were my favorite. It was just like the one Mary Lennox used to open the gate in *The Secret Garden*, the one she hoped would save her from the grief of abandonment and bring a whole new world to life.

I held tight to the key, and that night I tucked myself into bed hating myself and praying that God would take away my desire to be with a woman.

# 6

## DATING DISSONANCE

Not long after Jason, I left the daycare and found a new job. I wanted a new start. Wiping snotty noses wasn't making me happy, so I found something that would: a coffee shop, the natural Mecca of progressive-minded young latte-sippers. Unfortunately, this new pond still yielded no fish. Not that soulmate searching was my sole objective, though. I thought about it, yes, but my life didn't revolve around the possibility of finally crossing paths with Mr. Right. Hell, I was just actively hoping to be attracted to someone with that prefix.

Perhaps therein lurked my problem. Every shift at the coffee shop yielded hundreds of patrons, many of whom were eligible bachelors. The quaint little cafe also naturally selected my style of partner, or what I *thought* to be my type. Slender guys wearing bowties, guys who knew the difference between a latte and a cappuccino, poetry-wielding guys with plastic frame glasses who treated the local coffee shop like another accessory to their style. I loved looking at them, but I wanted nothing more than to take their pretentious coffee orders and smile bashfully. It was like going to a zoo and admiring the tigers for their stunning stripes but knowing good and well I didn't want to take one home. I appreciated the aesthetics as a "normal" girl should, but then quickly became disinterested—something my mom continuously attributed to my self-deprecating lack of confidence.

My interest in relationships seemed to decay before it ever blossomed. Was my approach wrong? Perhaps I was being smothered by meeting people in person. I considered the online dating craze and entertained the whim for a mere four seconds before scoffing at it. But when my own parents suggested it, I thought, *What do I have to lose?* Perhaps my mom was right. Maybe a more detached approach to dating was more my style. In a joking manner, my parents said they wanted to give me a gift card for one of the popular sites. The suggestion, though partially in jest, seemed rather genuine. In a moment of desperation, I took them up on the offer.

The next afternoon, I found myself typing in the digits of my dad's credit card and signing up for three months of soulmate surfing. The personality profile tests and empty boxes were beyond daunting. I didn't feel interesting enough to fill them with vivid and enthralling aspects of myself, nor was I ready for what personalities those mini monologues would attract. How truly accurate was the depiction of my spirituality when I had to rank religious importance on a scale of "not very" to "highly"? Well, of course, my spirituality was highly important, vital even, but would this attract men who expected me to be submissive, wear a denim jumper, and only see G-rated movies?

Ultimately, I went with gut instinct and decided to let spirituality play a role in matching me with the right person. It was God's jurisdiction anyway, right? Was I usurping God's role by even *partaking* in online dating? I tried to quell the philosophical meanderings of my mind and just answer the questions. I looked at the dried crust of my long-abandoned lunch and realized the sandwich shop where I had been building (no, obsessing over) my dating profile was about to close for the evening.

Over the next few weeks, I refreshed the mobile dating application on my phone a thousand times. The progression of communication was absurd, really. Having to wink, poke, like, and answer canned questions with each match before actually sending real-life messages drained me by the time a normal conversation began. I went on dates with several guys, ranging from spiritual interrogator to Iron Man competitor. Each one left me in a lurch of disinterest and avoidance.

The customary dinner dates, twenty questions, feigning interest, and awkwardly reaching for checks became a song and dance I eventually set to auto pilot. Acting as if I had completely dematerialized after the first date became my specialty. I avoided texts, calls, and messages until the pursuer contacted me with an exasperated resignation, to which I never responded but rather moved to the next recipient of hurt. I'm not proud of it.

At the time, I was blogging about new adventures in this new city, and I remember writing a post entitled "Laugh at My Expense: Confessions of an Online Dating Subscriber." In it, I chronicled the process, using humor as a way to smooth the edges of a sharp reality, a reality that I didn't even know needed to be confronted. I tried to do what was best for my writing and tell stories in their most honest form, but what was the use of being transparent for an audience when I couldn't even be authentic with myself? Instead of using the experience to examine myself, I let it break my spirit. I ended with a cold and lonely statement. It read: *Needless to say, online dating did not work for me. What did I expect when I asked a computer to find love? Love can't be Googled. Love can't be matched. Love must be found. And honestly, I've stopped looking.*

As I re-read the blog recently, I ached for that writer. She was alone, confused, and longing to make a connection. The setting was seemingly perfect. An active, thriving, artsy town teeming with young, eligible people was indeed a great setting to meet someone, and perhaps widening the parameters with online dating was the answer. But instead, I felt like a solitary bird in a cage. My setting was the same—a place in which I was merely an onlooker, barred by invisible barriers and trapped in my own enclosure of sorts. I was years away from being released.

I deactivated my profile and moved on.

# 7

## THAILAND

And by move on, I literally mean that I moved to the other side of the globe and embarked on a new adventure. I had recently met my best friend, Kelsey, and after finding out that our Alma Maters and humor were the same, we became fast friends. Both eager to travel, we planned a teaching excursion to Thailand. It was a way to help me leave confusion and indecision behind. With a worn copy of *Eat, Pray, Love,* I boarded a fourteen-hour flight away from my doubts, disappointments, and the fear that told me I would never find the type of love I so genuinely craved. For a year, I lived in a northern province of Thailand called Uttaradit, with Kelsey, my dearest and best friend from college. Together, we taught English as a second language, expanded our palates with decadent, spicy foods, and watched elephants walk the streets. It was like stepping into a completely different world—in every sense of the term. New terrain, harsh weather, odd flavors, and beautiful customs welcomed us every day. The experience detached me from my worries, as well as from the comfort zone of my traditional Southern upbringing.

One of the most glaring differences I saw upon entering this new culture was its gender fluidity. I was accustomed to staunch gender roles and a great divide between guys and girls—regarding everything from what colors to wear, to what toys to play with, to which people we were allowed to love. In striking contrast, heterosexual PDA was discouraged in Thailand, while same-sex affection was nearly paraded. Whether or not these partnerships were romantic didn't matter. This custom still paved the way for Thais who identified as LGBT to explore their sexuality without being ashamed. I never saw anything but pride when it came to my students' expression of themselves and their identities. I saw straight high school boys hold hands in the school courtyard. I saw girls being "gentlemen" toward other girls.

One day I mustered up the courage to ask a fellow English teacher, "Why do the dress codes and haircut rules not apply to that girl?" I nodded discreetly toward a student in my all-girl class who definitely didn't fit the customary description. They were all seventh graders.

"This one identifies as a Tom, see?" Without hesitation, the teacher asked her to stand. After a Thai phrase or two, the student's eyes smiled and she nodded vigorously. "I asked her if she was a Tom. Simple as that." He shrugged. "They're not shy about it."

The spectrum in Thailand was broad but very qualifiable (and evidently un-closeted). There was even a chart to help me understand the wide array of sexualities, complete with helpful arrows that indicated who was usually attracted to whom. "Toms" were tomboy females (attracted exclusively to women) who adopted male roles, dress, styles, and habits. "Dees" were women who visually passed as straight but only dated Toms. There were also "ladyboys" who, by nearest definition, fit our drag queen label. These were all somewhat familiar to me, but I'd never heard of the "Cherry" female before. These were straight women who were only attracted to gay men. For obvious reasons, that doesn't seem like a match made in nirvana, but Cherry couples existed nonetheless. The fluidity with which these (and many more categories) interacted was fascinating. Thai *acceptance* of these identities was even more mind-blowing.

Meanwhile, even after seeing all these liberating displays of sexuality, I was still hanging on to my last thread of hetero identification. Kelsey was successfully reviving a relationship back in the States, so I thought I might revisit a semi-relationship of mine as well. Spoiler alert: Kelsey's transcontinental love revival ended in blissful marriage, while mine ended with me realizing that I was most definitely gay. I struck up a conversation with a guy I had casually dated back home, and we started talking again over email. It was weird, and frankly, I'm not even sure why he responded. Our interactions at home had been so lackluster, so non-romantic. He had made several subtle attempts, but every time he would lean in for the kiss, I either dodged or rolled up the window. I even left the country in the middle of whatever we were—an awkward friendship at best. Why he emailed me back, I have no idea.

For several months, I was excited to see his messages in my inbox. Our emails were long and detailed, tinged with sarcasm and uneasy attempts to be sweet to one another again. I would painstakingly address all his quirky comments in parallel to his message. When I was done typing, my email was pretty much a mirror image of his. We never made any real progress in conversation, largely due to my inability to reciprocate any semblance of affection. We eventually began sending each other small (yet thoughtful) gifts in the mail. At least this took away the obligation to write a novella-length email. It also took packages three weeks to make the trip, so the turnaround time was more my speed in regards to communication with boys.

Near the end of my teaching contract in Thailand, I got a package from him. It was unmistakably record-shaped. I ripped open the box to find Judy Garland's greatest hits. I loved Judy Garland. I had all her movies, proudly displayed photo-biographies on my coffee table, and spouted fun facts about her anytime I could. As a kid, I had loved *The Wizard of Oz* and her version of "Have Yourself a Merry Little Christmas"—despite the fact that they were, respectively, bizarre and melancholy. The older I got, the more interested I became in her personal life and its many tragedies. She was a child performer who was run ragged by MGM studios, cranking out half a dozen movies per year while being ridiculed for being "overweight" and having a "less-than-ideal" nose. My heart broke to read about her many failed relationships, drug use, and unreliability on the movie set. She was the product of a machine that made her perform like a puppet but told her she wasn't good enough. Studying the life of Judy Garland helped me to navigate others' circumstances with grace and be more empathetic about where a person's shortcomings were rooted.

Judy meant so much to me. But did this boy understand that? Had we even talked about that, or did I just mention that I liked her in passing? My feelings collided, and my throat tightened. I was elated by the gift, but the disillusionment I felt toward the gift-giver made me want to throw the record out the window to be stomped on by an elephant. I wanted to know what it felt like to be given a sentimental gift by someone I loved. How *overjoyed* I would be.

The longer our fake repartee lasted, though, the more I had come to realize that I just liked the communication and the *project* of mustering feelings for a guy. Every so often, a warm feeling toward him would float through my heart, but as ardently as I tried to hang on, the feeling faded even faster, like a wisp of smoke from an extinguished candle. And that was just it—my energy trying to like him (and all other guys) was absolutely spent.

When I got home, we met up for coffee *once*. After that, I was done.

Everything before Thailand felt like standing in a puddle. I knew the texture of life, but I'd never been *immersed* in it. Living away from home plunged me into a depth I'd never experienced. I perceived differently, I was challenged differently, and I was surrounded by a wholly new environment. It was at this point, mostly subconsciously, that I began to realize that my customs weren't the only ones in existence—and perhaps I didn't have to be customary.

# 8

## IN-BETWEEN

I had been back in the States for a while, tossing around ideas of more traveling or perhaps graduate school, but mostly, I was reeling from the disorientation of my return home. As elated as I was to be home, I was equally frustrated by people's lack of understanding regarding the life I had lived in Thailand. Readjusting to narrower points of view, the concept of necessity versus luxury, and the simple idea of traveling beyond the Mason-Dixon line were all topics of conversation too deep for me to handle. Heap all of those things on top of the social pressures which awaited me, and I was experiencing more culture shock in Alabama than the first time I used a squatty-potty in Thailand.

Life for me had completely changed. I went from an overflowing sense of fulfillment regarding my job in Thailand back to an "in-between" phase working at the front desk of a gym. Even my family's church situation had changed while I was away. Talk about culture shock. Imagine my surprise, and later my relief, to find that my mom had migrated from the Baptist Church. It was a pivotal step in realizing that imperialistic proselytizing had poisoned my mind. I will admit, I was very uncomfortable the first time I went into an Episcopal church. People bowed, knelt, and crossed themselves a lot, and because I was never sure exactly what phrases signaled all the motions, I usually declined on all the above. Communion concerned me too because I had a pretty finicky palate where alcohol was concerned, and there was no *way* I was drinking after all of those people. And the hymns were only a tiny bit livelier than funeral dirges. Those were my only concerns, though.

My dull, dehydrated Baptist roots were transplanted and placed into a new and orderly service where scripture, prayers, readings, and sermons were more like lovely recitations than fiery chastisements. People even talked about taking care of animals and the environment. The services were beautifully repetitive, and the sermons were refreshingly concise and inclusive. My dad had been reluctant to join (though he had been born into the Catholic faith), my sister worked on Sundays, and I was elsewhere traveling when my mom made the refreshing leap to a denomination on the other side of protestantism. She was devout and dedicated, often times going to services on her own and being edified by the inclusive, authentic parishioners. After my travels, and after much persuasion, I decided to go to the Episcopal church on a regular basis, mainly just for my mom. I loved watching her participate, knowing exactly when to perform the sign of the cross, bow, and sing songs that weren't even in the hymnal. Though I felt out of place at first, I was comforted by her sense of calm and renewal. Perhaps it also inadvertently had me believe that she would be more open when she found out that I was gay.

# 9

## SEEKING

Seldom would I revisit something failed, but four years later, after having literally traveled around the world without so much as a glimpse of romance, I dusted off the pages of my online dating profile. This time, though, joining a dating website was not at the behest of my parents. It was because of my own discouragement. Societal pressure, exacerbated by social media posts about engagements and weddings, had compressed my heart so that it was almost numb, and I could not understand why I was unable to feel. Perhaps I wasn't ingrained with a romantic drive, or maybe I was being called by God to remain single. Depressing as the possible reasons were, disinterest and impending solitude were the only options I allowed my heart to claim. In a last-ditch effort to defy and disturb the reluctance in my mind, I paid $75 to cyberspace—money I didn't really have.

I confirmed my credit card number and was taken to the first page of the personality profile. My mouse hovered over the first question on the screen, and it reignited the very thing I had worked so long to suppress. What was I seeking? I felt a hesitance I had never experienced before. I knew what I *had been* looking for, but what I had been looking for felt all wrong and acted as merely a bandaid to what I was yearning to find. Would I be honest enough to allow what I was truly seeking to manifest itself outwardly? Could I take that first step?

And so, here I was at that familiar and terrifying crossroad. I held my breath and clicked. I am a woman seeking a man. *There shouldn't be another option*, my trained, fundamentalist mind lashed out. *I am supposed to select "man."* My swirling desire to click the alternative made me break out into a cold sweat, as if I had put my decision on public display by merely thinking it. To distract my mind, I spruced up my profile and refreshed it over and over again, hoping the new matches would distract me.

The obsession was unhealthy, really. It was as if I were waiting for a flashing marquee that read "This is the person God has chosen for you!" to pop up on the screen and alleviate all my worries and second-guessing. People often pray for signs from God, and because I had given up on that elusive "you just know" feeling long ago, I prayed the sign would be tangible, gaudy even. I knew that putting God in a box and asking that infinite wisdom be canned and prepared for human understanding was nonsensical and a bit bratty, but I was desperate.

Exhausted, I finally closed the dating app on my phone and set an alarm for church. As I drifted off to sleep, I prayed that I would meet someone. The fervency of that prayer rivaled that of my most hidden petitions, the ones in which I tried to "pray away the gay." But this time, I just prayed to be receptive. I even hoped that maybe, just maybe, I could experience that "just know" feeling.

When my alarm sounded the next morning, I sat up eagerly to check my profile. There were already several matches, but I didn't have time to thoroughly stalk my future mates until after church. I made coffee, let my greyhound out to potty, took a shower, and fried two eggs, as was my customary weekend morning routine. I lived within walking distance of my church. And when I say walking distance, I mean that it was literally one piece of property away from my townhouse complex. With five minutes to spare before the organ sang the processional tune, I grabbed my jacket and walked out into the brisk February air. Leaving any earlier would have forced me to be sociable with a church parish I hardly knew; I preferred slipping in with the acolytes and finding my seat discreetly. I didn't follow along in the bulletin, participate in readings, or sing the hymns, and I tried my best to remain as aloof as possible during the Peace, avoiding eye contact with most people besides my parents.

Perhaps that avoidance is why I hadn't noticed the new staff member at our church.

Perhaps my heart wasn't ready to meet her.

I had been too emotionally and spiritually unavailable to pay much heed when she was hired. I had vague recollections of the girl introducing herself to the church as the new youth minister earlier in the year, but that was all I knew. When people made announcements at church, I usually wriggled from view anyhow, placing a parishioner's head directly in the speaker's line of sight. I felt safer unnoticed.

When the last *Alleluia* was said, my family and I walked outside and began the usual Sunday afternoon debate on where to have lunch. Finally deciding to go see my sister, who served at a local restaurant in town, we headed to our respective vehicles. I began the stroll back to my house where my car was parked, carefully hewing a path away from fellow parishioners. As I walked away, though, I took notice of the youth minister interacting so effortlessly with the kids. My eyes lingered for a second. She was tall, with an authentic smile and striking eyes. I ducked out of view and continued home.

# 10

## MEETING LOVE

My greyhound nosed at the door and looked back at me with a forlorn, "I really have to pee" look. I had been trying my best to train her to give me an outward sign that she needed to go out, other than just plain peeing in the floor, so this was a step in the right direction. Only, I was a little peeved that she'd waited until I was out of my Sunday clothes and perched on the couch. I huffed. It had been a couple months since I began regularly attending the Episcopal church down the street, and I had acquired quite a routine. Apparently, so had my dog. Being a consistent and committed dog-owner, I leashed my pet and walked out into the mild February day, not bothering to put on shoes. Most often, Keeper peed only yards from my doorstep, but naturally on this day, she wanted to wander around in the brush. Pulling me relentlessly down the wooded property toward the church, my dog refused to find a suitable place to do her business. Patience hurt, and so did the acorns under my feet, but I traipsed dutifully along behind her.

Ahead in the clearing, I saw my church and was thankful all the cars were gone. Keeper nuzzled toward the perfectly arranged sod of the churchyard, and that's when I saw the lone car in the parking lot. Not wanting to socialize, I pulled my stubborn dog back in the direction of home. She would not budge. Then it was too late. I noticed a figure leaning into the back seat on the other side of the car, then feet began to move. Realizing that it was the new youth minister, I panicked and stared at the ground, hoping I'd suddenly become invisible. I tugged one last time at the leash, but my social dog, as indicted by her thrashing tail, had already seen the girl. And she was walking toward us. My heart rate accelerated. I awkwardly looked over my shoulder to see if she was somehow walking toward someone, anyone else.

"You must be Meredith!" she said in a lively tone. There was no mistaking that she was talking to me.

"Yeah!" I didn't know what else to say. I was suddenly hyper-aware of my shaggy and unkempt appearance.

"Would you happen to know where the dumpster is?" She was holding a plastic bag in her hand.

"No, I'm sorry," I said sheepishly yet suddenly eager to talk. "How did you know who I was?"

"Well, I saw you and your dog walking in the garden outside my office window this week, and I asked Father Michael if he knew who you were. . . I'm Allison."

"This is Keeper," I said, motioning toward my lanky dog, who was already introducing herself to the trash bag in her hand. In one swift move, Keeper latched on to the bag, locked her jaws, and began to pull. I was mortified.

Allison and I both fumbled around trying to procure the bag from my naughty, naughty dog. Finally, after several attempts to distract her, we snatched the trash bag away. I was flustered and embarrassed, but I would soon thank Keeper for this awkward introduction. After the trash fiasco, we began to chat about simple things like alma maters and hobbies, and before I even realized it, we were sitting in the grass talking about everything and nothing. I jabbered on and on, not even recognizing myself.

"Well, I'm going to Seattle and Portland for a week or so, but I'd love to hang out when I get back!" she said sincerely.

I was unprepared for my deep, inward reaction. I had already begun to miss her.

"What's the occasion up there?" I asked, shaking off my sudden disappointment.

"I'm going to a Human Rights Campaign conference," she replied.

Suddenly conflicted and feeling ignorant about what that meant, I simply said, "Cool!"

A thousand questions ran through my head. *Wait, isn't that the gay advocacy group? That can't be right. She works with the church, so she can't possibly be gay. Or support a gay organization. I'm sure there are gay ministers in Seattle, but not here. Is she going to learn how to cure people from being gay? But wait, is she gay? Why do I care so much?*

The sun was starting to set, and I was suddenly conscious that I'd been sitting in an ant pile. I swatted some of the pests away and looked at her, not wanting our conversation to end. Her lips pursed in a kind way, and her eyes were soft and inviting. I felt like telling her everything, but I stayed silent so I could hear her speak, hear her beautiful laughter, and soak in the gentleness that poured out even in the tilt of her eyebrows. The way she sat on the grass, legs folded daintily, and the way her short hair was whisked away by the February wind made me want to hold her hand. And I didn't know exactly why. All I knew was that I had finally looked into the tender, blue-eyed soul of a person who might be able to help pull me from a dreary fog. Already, I thought of that patch of grassy earth where we sat as hallowed.

Before I told her that I was crazy about her and wanted to spend every day thereafter in the rays of her gentleness, I simply said, "It was so nice to meet you!" Then a reluctant, "Goodnight."

# 11

## BOWLING

I let two days drag by before texting her. There weren't necessarily any rules because I wasn't even sure what was happening, but I didn't want to seem too eager, nonetheless. Dwelling way too long on how it might be perceived, I decided to send her a picture of my dog. Innocent enough, but it adequately expressed that I was thinking of her and masked the pining with nonchalance. I captioned the photo: *Keeper says hello!* Within minutes I got an enthusiastic response. Her name on my phone gave me an elated rush unlike any I had ever felt. After reading Allison's reply a dozen times, I left our conversation there—floating somewhere between fun new friend and perhaps more.

From the day I met Allison, no one else ever appeared on my radar. I saw no glances, heard no compliments, felt no stir of excitement aside from those associated with her. I was blissfully unaware of everyone else, yet hyper-aware of Allison and praying she felt the same.

A few days later, she sent me a photo of an old washer captioned, *Was running out of clean clothes. Finally found a laundromat!* Never had I seen such a beautiful washer. I wanted to print it, frame it, hang it on my wall, then shout to the rooftops that whatever this girl sent was thenceforth art. Dialing down the fervor, I replied accordingly.

The intermittent small talk went on for over a week. I wasn't sure when she got back from her Seattle trip, but I was hopeful that I would see or hear from her again soon. Holding in such excitement was so difficult. Imagine years deprived of gushing over a loved one, or countless anniversaries celebrated in loneliness rather than in love; I was bursting at the gills to catch up on all the time I'd lost being single and uncertain. But I couldn't risk revealing my true feelings to my friends and family. Not just feelings for Allison but feelings in general—that I was unconventional in my view of love.

One day while I was at work, she texted me. Overjoyed, I feigned needing a bathroom break and snuck to the stalls to see what it said. She wanted me to help chaperone a youth event at the bowling alley the following weekend. Well of course I would. I would've gone to a toaster repair seminar to be near her. But I questioned her motives. Was I just another helper? Or was this perhaps her way of asking to hang out and get to know me in a low-stress environment? Whatever the case, I was elated at the chance to see her again. When that Sunday afternoon came, I drove to the bowling alley tangled in a ball of nerves. I was a little late because I had changed outfits seven times, and I was pretty certain my newly applied swipe of deodorant was already wearing off. Not to mention, I was unsure how to interact with middle school church kids, and I was *definitely* unsure of how to act around the person who didn't know I liked her. What a pickle.

Twenty frames of bowling went by as I mingled in and amongst the youth. I tried to be helpful and monitor the kids, who thought it'd be funny to change fellow players' initials to something stupid and alter each other's scores. I was blissfully unaware; I didn't know the kids' names anyhow. Then suddenly, while I was poking around on the worn keys of the old bowling machine, I heard a crash followed by laughter. My head shot up from behind the computer like a meerkat from a dusty hole in the ground. When the kids cleared, I saw Allison flat on her back. One step too far into the greasy lane without proper shoes, and she was a goner. Thankfully, I saw her beautiful smile flash a few times, indicating that she'd not cracked her skull and was laughing off the fall like a champ. A concussion would not have been a good start to our first "perhaps-this-is-a-date."

As the youth event was coming to an end and everyone turned in their shoes to be disinfected, I scrambled to think of a way I could keep the night going. Since Allison had been on youth minister duty, we hadn't gotten to talk much. As we said goodbye to the last kid being picked up, I nervously put my hands in my pockets and lingered by the door where Allison stood. She smiled, and we walked out together.

"So what do you want to do now?" she asked happily, as if she had planned all along to spend more time with me.

"Umm, I don't know!" I replied, smiling sheepishly. "Dinner, drinks? Where would you like to go?"

"I still haven't learned a lot about this town," she admitted, "so wherever you suggest!"

I was no expert at making social plans, but I quickly took the reins so as not to lose this opportunity. "I know a great place downtown. Follow me!"

Sunday evening on Broad Street was less than lively. We parked our cars in front of Blackstone, the little pub whose colorful wall-murals made it an iconic spot in town. Being among the only people in the whole place, we had our choice of where to sit. I led us to a dimly lit table close to the shabby pool tables in the back. The table was round, small, intimate.

"What would you like to drink?" I asked.

"Let's see." She swiveled around in her chair to look at the selections on tap. "I'll have a Blue Moon."

"I got it!" I said, immediately jumping up and heading to the bar.

I was not a beer-drinker. Quite honestly, I didn't like alcohol much at all. Considering how much I was sheltered from it as a child (and even as a twenty-one year old), one would probably expect me to have dived head first into experimentation. Alcohol fell into three categories for me: too expensive, too much sugar, and tastes like horse pee (not that I'd ever tried horse pee, per se).

"What can I get for you?" asked the tattooed bartender.

"Two Blue Moons, please," I responded reluctantly. "Oh, and can you put a lot of extra orange slices in one? Thanks."

I returned to the table with the cold mugs, mine trimmed excessively with citrus. I pulverized every last drop from each slice hoping it would curb the peach-scented urine flavor. It was so obvious that I was out of my beer-connoisseurship league. A few quick sips were enough to soften the edge of my nerves, though, and I began to sink comfortably into our conversation. Allison was so smart and so full of life. The vibrancy in her voice was contagious, and though we talked later and later into the evening, I felt more and more enlivened with every new topic. A large pizza and a half a beer later (because I babysit my alcohol), we reached a lull in the conversation.

"Tell me about your tattoos," she said. "Can I see them?"

"The explanation is so involved," I replied timidly. "It would probably be best if I just gave you a pamphlet on them."

She laughed and said, "No, please! I want to hear everything."

Rolling up my sleeve, I walked her through the timeline of my tattoos and essentially told her about all the major benchmarks in my life that they represented. I told her about my first tattoo, the bird on my wrist that represented release and freedom. I had gotten that one in my tiny college town with the guy who had been my nightmarish first-kiss experience (the guy with the psychedelic room and iguana). I told her about the Victorian poetry script on the inside of my arm and how it symbolized spiritual uncertainly but, ultimately, peace with God's will. I told her about my cultural tattoos from Thailand. I told her about my half-sleeve filled with flight imagery, kaleidoscope discs, a postmarked envelope, and billowing clouds. The envelope even featured a term or two from an Episcopal advent devotional I'd done the Christmas before. Then I showed her the outline of Rosie the Riveter on the inside of my other bicep and took another brave step. It wasn't the few sips of beer talking either. It was just me being absolutely allured by her.

"I'm actually going to get this piece filled in with color next week. Would you like to join me?"

"That would be so much fun! Of course." She seemed sincerely excited.

"Great," I said, containing my excitement as I grabbed my warm beer. I took a minuscule sip and grimaced.

"You don't like beer, do you?" Allison asked with a knowing smile.

I caved. "It's disgusting."

"Here, I will take care of that for you." She took the pint glass and finished it off.

I adjusted my chair, crossed my legs again, and leaned on the table a bit closer than I had been before. Reciprocating her interest in me, I said, "Now, walk me through your life. Let's start with high school or college. I want to hear everything."

I propped my head in my hands and listened as she told me about summer camp, a liberal arts school in the mountains, a year off to advocate for a non-profit organization in California, her travels to Uganda, and youth ministry in Alabama. I etched notes in my head. I was so caught up in conversation, even the doubts in my mind, every bit of slander I'd heard from a pulpit, had quieted. I was falling so fast in love that every outside hindrance seeking to grab me was rushing past in a silent blur, and all I could see was her.

What seemed like moments later, I looked at my watch. It was after midnight, and Blackstone had closed two hours ago. Since the bartenders had let in a few friends and stayed for a private evening of billiards and drinks, no one had told us to scram.

"Oh my gosh," I said, looking up. "I have to be at work at five a.m."

"What? No! That's awful." Allison got up and started gathering her things. "I'm so sorry I kept you out so late."

"Please don't apologize. I have enjoyed this so much. I can take a nap tomorrow afternoon."

We walked out to our cars. The air was silent except for the humming street lamps. Not knowing exactly how to part ways, I stalled for a moment and fumbled around for my keys. I looked up, and Allison was already at her car door. No awkward side-hug, just an unceremonious goodbye.

# 12

## RUNNING FROM MY VOICE

Our small town didn't have a lot to offer in the "things to do" department. The situation was made even more complex as I tried to think of something fun that wouldn't exactly insinuate a date. Although, let's be real. In my heart, it was a date. My finger hovered over the call button, and I mustered the courage to ask her out on an another adventure (preferably without the youth group this time).

"Hi!" she answered quicker than I had anticipated. Hearing her happy voice made made my voice shaky.

I went out on a limb and asked her to come mountain biking with me. A leisurely walk, a coffee date, or a movie matinee were all safer bets, but I was obviously not conventional.

"I haven't really ever been mountain biking on actual trails, but I'm definitely willing to try!" Allison replied without a moment's hesitation. I was thrilled to hear the genuine interest she took in both me and my hobbies.

Later, I found out that it was more of an interest in *me*, and the mountain biking was merely the obstacle that accompanied it. Nonetheless, I had found someone who celebrated my interests with me no matter what.

Allison listened intently as I gave her basic riding instructions. I gave a mini demo, showing her how to balance her body above the bike, how to brake properly, and how to coast the downhills with her pedals at 9 and 3 so as not to scrape the rocks and roots. Perhaps this was too much information, but I was excited and chatty. We pedaled to the trail entrance, and I led the way. Allison followed close behind. I took the loop at a fair pace because the last thing I needed was to damage the girl I was crazy about. Periodically, as we wheeled around sharp switchbacks or took quick dips, I'd glance back and see her jaw clenched in concentration.

"Just keep pedaling and trust your tires to grab on," I called over my shoulder as we traversed a dry creek bed and made the last slow climb to the end.

We emerged from the wooded trail into the sunlight. I clamped down on my brakes, letting my rear tire skid and throw a cloud of dust as I wheeled around. Squinting to avoid the sudden brightness, I completed my turn to see Allison pedaling out of the woods. She looked exhilarated and a little tired, like a kid who'd just completed her first bike ride minus training wheels.

"That was so fun," Allison remarked as she unclipped her helmet. I hoped it wasn't obligatory. "But that was a lot harder than I imagined. I think one lap might be all I can handle today."

"Totally fine," I said, happy to stop on a good note. "You did a great job for it being your first time."

We walked the bikes back to my car in silence. It wasn't the awkward kind, but rather the kind of silence that allows you to rest in the comfort of just being together. It was easy from the very start.

"Hey, what would you say to joining me for dinner at my family's house tonight?" I blurted it out before I had the nerve to squash the idea.

This was a considerate and neighborly gesture, right? Not an "I want you to meet my family because this is serious" kind of move. Or was it? In a matter of milliseconds, my thoughts tumbled out of control. What if Allison and I worked out? What if I came out? My family might disparage my very being. Being an "us" in small town Alabama seemed terrifying and exhilarating. I had lived a life full of caution and hesitancy. Unbeknownst to everyone but myself, this tiny step of admitting affection was a huge breakthrough. Embarking on a journey like this, discovering what I truly wanted, was a thrill I'd never felt up until this point.

"Well that sounds like a pretty genuine offer to me," Allison replied. "I'd love to."

When we pulled into my family's driveway that evening, my stomach seemed to dive down into my shoes. I suddenly realized how many emotions and intentions I had to juggle. I didn't want my family to notice my googly-eyed smiles at Allison, but I also didn't want to treat her like my pat-on-the-back, buddy-ole-pal and have Allison think she was merely that. I took a breath, and we walked inside together.

Allison was greeted with hugs and compliments. My family, especially Mamaw, was always so loving toward newcomers. She was fascinated by new people, especially anyone new in my life, and she made exceptional efforts to make them feel as if they were long-lost family coming home from an extended stay away. My whole chest flickered with warmth as I watched Allison interact with them and carry on conversation. Her effortless communication was intriguing to watch. I buttered cornbread, watching her smile and engage with my family as if they were the only people who mattered. I held so tight to that moment because even then I knew that it wouldn't last.

"Oh, I just love your haircut," Mamaw said, complimenting Allison. "I wish I could get my hair to do that."

Besides her eyes, Allison's hair was one of the first aesthetic qualities I'd been wildly attracted to.

"Awww, thank you," was her reply. "That's so sweet. I really like your haircut too!"

So there was my family, complimenting Allison's hair, asking about her job with the church and her summers at camp. I basked in that calm moment and reached for another piece of cornbread. Even after we were done with dinner and coffee cake, we still sat gathered around the table. Both Mamaw and my mom were bragging on me as if *trying* to set us up.

"Have you heard Meredith sing?" Mamaw asked excitedly. She sighed. "Oh it's such a sweet voice. You should hear it"

"I have a recording of her on my phone!" Mom said, jumping up to grab it.

"Oh, Mom, no!" I said. My skin tingled with embarrassment. "It's not good. No, don't let her hear that."

But she ignored me, scrolling intently through the library of songs on her phone.

"Mom, really. I don't want her to—"

"Oh hush, it's great," she disregarded me, then continued to speak to Allison. "She wrote a blog a few years back about empowering women to feel capable of trying new things, so she stepped out of her comfort zone and recorded the sweetest song."

At this point, I was halfway down the hallway, mortified at the thought of Allison hearing me sing. I was not being very supportive of my own blog's argument, I realize, but this was an entirely different circumstance. I'd not summoned within myself the confidence to be so open with her yet. I knew (and hoped) it would eventually be a glorious process, but even this tiny display of myself was too painful. I was literally running down the hallway from my own voice. Perhaps this was all too foretelling of how grueling it would eventually be. I would soon voluntarily reveal a truth from which I could not run. I couldn't escape down the hallway like a child, covering my ears, thinking that if I couldn't hear the reaction, it didn't exist.

After a feasible enough time had passed, I crept back down the hall toward the kitchen. My mom and Mamaw were washing dishes, and Allison still sat at the table, her back to me. When I came into the room, she turned around quickly and smiled. There were tears in her eyes.

"That was so beautiful, Meredith," she said.

And I knew everything would be all right.

# 13

## SNOW DAY

Chilly fall weather brings the promise of fun holidays ahead, but the cold can get a little dreary after Christmas—a reminder of the daunting new year begun, followed by the dreaded single's awareness day. Though I would choose the cold over summer any day, my post-holiday slump has always been pretty oppressive. The only consolation, says my inner child, would be a snow day—not just a dusting, but a shut-down-the-town kind of blanketing. That wasn't necessarily an out-of-reach proposition in our southern town, where even the threat of snow would sometimes shut down the city.

The clouds were especially billowy that day, and contrary to expectation, the temperature wasn't staggeringly low. I'd been home from work for a while and was planning to take my scheduled nap. Being naturally reclusive, I never opened my curtains or blinds; I preferred dark, enclosed spaces. Imagine my abundant surprise (for an abundance of reasons) when I saw that Allison was calling, and I wasn't in the least upset that my nap time had been derailed.

"Look outside!" she called to me with childlike excitement. "It's snowing!"

I pulled open the blinds to see snow blanketing the ground. In the short time I had been home, the billowy clouds had dumped such a thick layer of snow that the ground, rooftops, and cars were already completely covered. My first thought was to pray it stuck overnight so as to prohibit my commute to work. There was a pretty solid chance in a town so unprepared for wintry mixes of any kind. And this was more snow than the infamous Blizzard of '93. That's right, our snow experiences were so scarce, we *named* them.

"This came out of nowhere," I replied. "I had no idea!"

"I'm next door at the church right now. You should come over so we can play in it!"

My heart warmed at the genuinely playful pitch in her voice, and because she'd asked me to join her. In a matter of minutes, I'd thrown on a layer of clothes, rubber boots, and my favorite knit toboggan. I traipsed down the street toward the churchyard, where I found Allison taking photos of the snow-capped church. It looked like something from a magazine. The wooden, A-frame building was nestled in a patch of trees that seemed to isolate it from the busy road nearby. It was a place where I would always feel safe. Allison knelt down, shifted angles, snapping dozens of shots as I approached her.

"Hi!" I called to her, having decided that throwing a snowball wasn't the best greeting choice at this point in our relationship.

"Hi!" she called back. "It's a snow day!"

We frolicked around the churchyard like children, the snow piling quickly from barely a light dusting to a winter wonderland. It was our duty to play. Our first inclination was to build a snowman, of course, but not the customary, three-tiered variety. We decided to make our own version of Olaf from Disney's recent smash-hit movie.

"Let's build him on the church steps," Allison suggested, already piling a bit of snow for the foundation.

"Are you sure Father Michael will be okay with that?" I asked.

"Oh, Michael doesn't mind at all," Allison assured me. "Olaf will be an awesome greeter."

Armful after armful, stair-climb after stair-climb, we constructed the oblong base. Although fun, the snow-person quickly became a serious art project. We were all in. Using numb fingers, we scrolled through countless images on our phone in search of the perfect one to replicate, dug in the frozen shrubbery bed for contouring dirt, and extracted only the best twigs for Olaf's expressive arms. Chunks of his head kept falling off, but we persevered.

"We don't have a carrot though," I said, standing back to take a look at the almost finished project.

"Hmm, I could check inside the church," Allison said. "Or we could go ask some neighbors for a carrot."

We were both silent for a second.

"Oh well," Allison said, letting go of the idea. "Let's go make snow angels and move on with our lives."

Finding a patch of perfectly pristine snow in the parking lot, we carefully sat down and stretched out our limbs. I was immediately soaked. I looked over, and through my cumbersome jacket, scarf, and toboggan combo, I could see Allison's long frame gliding over the frozen ground. Red nose and cheeks peeked from her jacket hood, and I could see that she was smiling. It was a perfect day. We gingerly escaped from our snow-angel outline, careful not to cause even the slightest blemish. Allison took out her phone and snapped a few pictures of the angel couple.

"Ugh, my phone ran out of space," she said.

"Don't worry about it. I have mine!" I was glad to help. This was also an opportune time to maybe get a photo of us. I delicately suggested, "How about we take a selfie too! With Olaf in the background?"

"Yeah!" was her enthusiastic agreement.

We trudged back to the church steps. The wind and snow were steadily picking up. I turned on my front-facing camera, and positioned Olaf in perfect photo-bombing position. My fingers were numb and burned when I attempted to press the button to snap the picture.

"Keep smiling," I said through clenched teeth, hoping I was getting some good ones. I quickly scrolled through them, my heart swelling to see what I hoped would be the first of many photos together. When I put my phone in my pocket, there was a stalled moment in which I wondered what was happening next.

"So, I probably shouldn't drive in this weather," Allison said cautiously, but with an overtone that suggested she might like to stay over. Allison lived about an hour away and only came to town a few days per week for work.

"You're welcome to stay with me! We can watch movies and make breakfast for dinner."

"That sounds great!" Allison seemed just as enthusiastic about the slumber party as I was.

So we walked home and began our first evening together. It felt so right to see her in my kitchen scrambling eggs and telling me stories. She told me about her year of political advocacy at a non-profit in San Diego, about sleeping outside a senator's office, about her sisters and the border collies she'd had as a kid. She leaned against the refrigerator as I made omelets and biscuits. I looked back once and caught her glance in mine. She truly looked at home.

# 14

## OVER THE RAINBOW

That afternoon, Allison indulged my love of old movies, and we began watching *Meet Me in St. Louis*, an old MGM film starring Judy Garland.

Earlier that day I'd waxed poetic about my affinity for old movies. Looking back, it was glaringly obvious that I was head-over-heels for this girl, or in keeping with the theme, I was "over the rainbow" for her.

"Brown Avenue," Allison mentioned as she passed the street sign by the church, "has got to be the most dull avenue in Rainbow City."

I had never before thought twice about the quirky name of our little town, but since she mentioned it, my mind whirled around and landed on one of my favorite movies. "Fun fact," I said, testing the waters, "conjecture is that the rainbow flag originated from Judy Garland's earliest film, *The Wizard of Oz*."

"Is that so?" Allison said matter-of-factly. There was a cute expression in the corners of her mouth.

"Yeah," I said excitedly and continued. "Judy was such an open and supportive advocate of the gay community and the arts. She had several accompanists who were gay, and she herself was even rumored to have had a romantic relationship with a woman at one point." I paused. *Too much?*

"Cool," Allison responded with eyebrows slightly raised, insinuating I go on.

"Judy became synonymous with safety during these closeted times, and her song *Somewhere Over the Rainbow* quickly became a gay anthem," I shrugged. "Or so the story goes."

Way later in our relationship, Allison revealed that my not-so-subtle Judy Garland story was the answer to her final suspicions about my sexuality. Thus began a lovably awkward and unsure adventure toward being us.

As we sat together, I was very aware of our proximity to one another. My couch was a puffy loveseat that tucked two people very comfortably into its velvety cushions, making it very difficult for limbs not to be touching. Wrapped tight in a blanket and clinging to the edge, I tried to act natural. As much as I wanted to cozy up beside her, I didn't yet have the guts to let myself reveal such an intimate desire, much less go out on a limb to see if she felt the same. Instead of overthinking, I tried to just enjoy her company, and every once in a while, watched as the television's light hit the already familiar angles of her face.

The snow day caught up to us quickly, though. Barely halfway into the film, we both agreed it was time for sleep. I made sure she had adequate blankets and pillows, grabbed the dog, and wished her goodnight before going to my room. I paused, holding my door open just a little so I could see through the crack. She got settled, and I heard a comfortable sigh reassuring me that her long legs weren't too cramped on the short couch. Falling asleep that night, I said a prayer that God would have her stay.

■ ■ ■

I was awakened the next morning by Keeper pacing around the room. I knew she had to pee, but I wasn't about to go through the living room and wake up Allison. After letting Keeper out the back door, I brushed my teeth, checked my social media accounts, and even drifted back to sleep for a little while. I'd not heard any movement from the other room yet, but I was feeling anxious. What if she had to use the bathroom and was afraid to knock on my door? Would it be nice if I made her coffee? What if she would rather I not grind coffee beans and wake her up? What if I was wasting my energy and she didn't even care about me? These and many more questions had me pacing until I finally decided to open the door and have a peek. The hinges squeaked, and Keeper's long nose nuzzled through the opening in an attempt to escape and find the new friend in the house. Her dog tags banged against the doorframe, and I saw Allison's head pop up over the back of the couch.

"I'm so sorry to wake you!" I said apologetically.

"You didn't! I was already awake and waiting for you to get up."

After coffee, we put our dry snow clothes back on and took a walk around the neighborhood. The town had fallen silent at the behest of the snow, so we zig-zagged freely down the middle of the street. Of course Allison had her camera. I was enthralled, watching her examine even the tiniest of snow-dusted things. Thorn bushes, paw prints, red berries, rooftops, and boughs were all her subjects. Walking alongside her, I fought the constant compulsion to grab her hand.

We had reached a comfortable seam in our time together. The morning waned, the snow was beginning to melt, and Allison decided it was best if she headed home. The very moment she left, I took out my phone and scrolled through the photos we had taken together the day before. My frozen fingers had captured dozens of images, chronicling our laughter. I chose my favorite one, edited the contrast, and let my hands type out a basic caption. When I pressed "post," though, I was making a personal declaration. I was introducing her to the world as my person. It was written all over my face.

# 15

## ROSIE THE RIVETER

The outline of my Rosie the Riveter tattoo had healed, and my color fill-in appointment finally arrived. Although I had mentioned the appointment to Allison the night at Blackstone Pub, I was pessimistically sure she had forgotten. She was busy, I told myself, most likely with a social life that far outweighed mine in all its lackluster glory. Self-doubt had me type out, almost send, and delete several messages to her before building the proper confidence to ask her to join me. When I did finally text her, she responded almost immediately.

*Yeah, I would love to join you! I'm at a coffee shop with my sister, but just let me know when you get into town! I'm excited to be your tattoo cheerleader.*

I spent the next hour getting ready and finding just the right "I really care, but I don't want you to know" outfit. I put on just enough makeup to accentuate my eyes, but not enough to seem unnatural. I sprayed perfume in all the places magazines suggested, took a deep breath, and walked out the door. I had nearly an hour drive to calm my nerves and theorize how the evening would go. When I got closer to town, she gave me the address to her place. As the mileage on my directional app ticked away, I got more and more nervous. Our time together kept seeming more and more like dates. When I arrived, Allison met me outside. She greeted me with a close hug, and I tried desperately not to sink too comfortably into her arms.

"Ready for tattoo time?" she asked enthusiastically.

"Yeah!" I really was pretty excited to finally see Rosie with a red bandana.

"Do they hurt as bad as I'm imagining they do?" she asked with a grimace.

"It feels like a very irritating scratch," I said, "but the longer the session, the more painful it gets. You might even have to hold my hand."

I didn't know how or why that sentence came out of my mouth, but a prickly chill ran down my spine, wondering how she would perceive that statement. I tried to dismiss how awkward I felt, but Allison didn't seem to miss a beat. I hoped that meant she wasn't uncomfortable. Then again, I was feverishly over-analyzing our conversations without knowing at what angle she was approaching the situation. Maybe she was still in the "friend zone" and didn't think a thing about the hand-holding comment. It wouldn't be much longer before I found out.

When we pulled up to the tattoo studio, I was visibly nervous and grateful that the imminent needle pricks were adequate cover for my anxiety. I sat in the chair as the artist cleaned my arm and set out his palette. Allison watched closely, seemingly intrigued by the craftsmanship he showed as he assembled the tattoo gun and mixed various colors. His foot pumped on the sewing machine–style pedal and he buzzed the needle around in the ink. The red dye quivered.

"Ready?" He asked, grinning through his lumberjack beard.

"Go for it," I said.

Allison reached for my hand and held it tight as the needle began filling in Rosie's polka-dot bandana. The buzzing gun, the irritating sting, and the loud music vanished as my focus narrowed to only her hand. I focused so intently that I could nearly feel the curved ridges of her fingerprints. I brushed my fingers lightly back and forth across hers, and I think that's when she knew.

Rosie the Riveter represented so much about the person I had tried to become: a strong, competent, independent woman stepping up to the plate and filling an unprecedented role. It wasn't until I had acquired this Rosie-esque individualism that I was able to be open and honest with myself. For so long, I had ignored the yearnings of my heart, the ache to understand the difference between fixation and love. I relentlessly sought people and relationships I thought would work simply because they fit a mold of what I *should* want. I obsessed over the pursuit, but when it came to cultivating a relationship, I ran. Trapped inside a conventional box, I was conditioned to view people mechanically, as lists of attributes society deemed to be well-matched for me. So, I treated love like a scavenger hunt, not the effortless merging of hearts it should be. The transference of Rosie onto my skin, the tangible commemoration of her ideals seemed to transpose all that I had ever known (and didn't know) about love, and the moment Allison held my hand was the moment I accepted who I was. The restraints of my obsession, my worry and doubt, were released, and I was able to run, without bounds, to the limitless depths of affection.

I'm sure my tattoo artist was smirking and rolling his eyes beneath those unruly eyebrows. I'd flown solo in the parlor several times already, and was no stranger to the discomfort of tattoos. I'd sat for hours like a champ, never before *needing* a hand to hold. This feeling with Allison there was wholly different. I *wanted* a hand to hold. It was this juxtaposition of thought that I struggled to understand at first: the difference between wanting someone and needing someone. A month or so down the road, (spoiler alert) after Allison and I began dating, I mentioned this idea of needing her. We were still new at togetherness, and day by day we figured out more and more about one another, but I was a little taken aback when she didn't agree.

"Don't you think it's healthier to want to be part of someone's life rather than it be a necessity?" she asked. "I don't *need* you in order to continue living, but I want you. And honestly," she paused, "I would find that more desirable."

Except for an acknowledging *hmmm*, I was quiet as I sat beside her. Was it bad that I wanted to feel needed? I mulled this over for a long time afterward, trying to grasp what was more desirable. In my mind, things that mattered were needed. After finally finding someone who made me feel like I mattered, I couldn't understand why that couldn't be equated with need. I wanted to mean the world to her, just like she did to me.

Soon I began to understand. Our needs are like involuntary actions, things we don't necessarily put a lot of thought into—like breathing, or our hearts pumping blood through our bodies. But the achievements and careers and people we *want* are the facets of life we pursue and the ideas in which we invest all our thoughts. When my mind wants to wander and daydream, I think of Allison because I *want* to. I didn't really make the decision to breathe today, but I did make the decision to love. Effortlessly, vastly, and without limitation, I *wanted* to love her. Free of labels, auto-piloted demands, and requirements, I *chose* to love her. Ironically enough, it was in the tattoo parlor that the embodiment of this "want versus need" concept was so apparent. And it was in those same moments that I felt the purest form of desire: the choice to love someone with my whole heart.

■ ■ ■

I was almost disappointed when Rosie was finished so quickly and I had to let go of Allison's hand. The time had been so sweet. We'd talked, made jokes, laughed, and held eye contact longer than we ever had before. The artist coated Rosie with ointment and wrapped her snuggly with plastic wrap, leaving my arm sidelined for tasks like juggling my things and putting on my seatbelt. Allison kindly assisted me, and we made our way back to her place. It was getting really late, but I didn't want to leave just yet.

"Want to come inside and see my apartment?" she asked as we pulled into the drive.

"Sure!" I replied, glad to have a reason to stay.

The old hardwood floors creaked beneath our feet as we walked inside. The building was dated, but its features and its placement in such a hip area of town gave it a beautiful authenticity. As with most older layouts, the space was plentiful and flowing. Allison turned on the lights in her art room.

"I got this on the side of the road," she said, motioning to a large, sturdy table full of paint-smattered plates and colorful brushes.

"I can't say that I've ever gotten anything off the side of the road before."

"Most of my things I've acquired from yard sales, antique stores, or just lucky discoveries on the side of the road. Life has been rather transient since college, so I've not made huge investments."

"I think all these pieces have such personality," I said, looking around with great interest.

Old suitcases were arranged on ladder-like shelving. Old letters, stamps collections, black and white photos, and paintings were grouped together in such clean ways. A painting of Alabama, quotes from the civil rights movement, and simply the word "yes" adorned various up-cycled pieces of wood and framing. Small, medicinal jars holding succulents and four-leaf clovers served as book-ends to classics like *The Awakening* and *Lord of the Rings.* Nostalgic political buttons and photos were tucked neatly along a framed piece of chicken wire, and flower pots were scattered here and there. Hues of light blue and occasional greens graced nearly every piece of art. Even the brush-rinsing jars were a cloudy blue. I absolutely loved her style.

"I don't have a couch right now, so there's not place really to sit," Allison confessed.

"It's no problem. I need to hit the road soon anyhow. It's getting late."

We continued the tour despite my obligatory "I must be going" statement, and she led me into her room. I felt a little uneasy at first, but I liked getting a closer look at her interior life. Allison opened her closet door, and there, taped in a beautiful collage, were dozens of hand-written notes, funny letters, silly drawings, and slips of fortune cookie papers.

"These things mean the most to me," she said. "More than anything else I own."

My heart swelled at her appreciation for words. I stood there and read the many sentiments from friends, summer camp kids, and family, all reiterating the things I'd already seen to be true about Allison—that she was gentle, loving, and had a heart for justice. Allison stood suspiciously close to me, appearing to reminisce and read the letters along with me. I took my time poring over each one, but I was nearly done and I didn't know what to do with myself. My stomach fluttered and my heartbeat sped up.

"I should probably be going," I said, awkwardly grabbing my sore, tattooed arm.

"Yeah, of course!" Allison said. "I'm sorry to have kept you so late. Do you need some coffee or anything for the drive home?"

I didn't necessarily need the caffeine, but I saw this as another way to extend our time together. "Yeah that would be helpful. What's open?"

We drove separately to a Waffle House down the street, where we waited for a fresh pot to brew. Our eyes were tired but happy as we walked in silence back out to our cars. I removed the lid, and blew some steam from the piping hot coffee. It warmed my face against the chilly night air. Allison gave me detailed directions on how to get back to the interstate, and we stood talking even longer about plans to hang out again.

"How about Sunday after church we get Thai food and have a movie marathon afternoon," I suggested.

"That sounds perfect." Allison smiled. "But there may need to be napping involved."

We stood a little closer than normal. Perhaps because it was cold, or dark, or because it was 1 a.m. on a dimly lit street. We lingered a little longer still. Perhaps because I was reluctant to make the long drive home. Then we hugged a little tighter. Perhaps because we knew we were both crazy about each other.

# 16

## I KISSED A GIRL, AND
## I LIKED IT

Sunday couldn't arrive fast enough. I'm ashamed to say that I was a little distracted during the church service that day. I'd never been head-over-heels before, though, so I hoped God would understand. My hopeful petitions had most likely been clogging the prayer highway, so I'm almost sure God was glad to have me preoccupied. After the last *go in peace to love and serve the Lord* rang out, I walked upstream through the crowd of people to find Allison. She was always inundated by parents asking questions about upcoming youth events, so I just touched her elbow gently and mouthed the words, *see you soon.*

For the first time in my life, I found myself looking forward to a potential romantic encounter with exhilaration. Prior to meeting Allison, I'd cornered myself into nausea-inducing apprehension before every date. I regretted talking to that guy in the pharmacy and making plans for dinner. I wished I could permanently wipe off that compulsory kiss or delete that silly dating profile. The idea of it all was so fun, but when it came down to it, I dreaded the follow-through. On the other hand, awaiting time spent with Allison made me well up with delight like a kid leaping from bed on Christmas morning. This opposite feeling was so foreign, and I was almost glad life had withheld it for so long because I was able watch it happen, name it, and embrace it as something altogether wonderful. Like the woodland creatures in Bambi, I was irrevocably twitterpated.

There was a knock on my door later that afternoon. I was dozing on the couch but hopped up, full attention. I darted to the mirror to check my hair, then raced back to the door. I took a glimpse through the peephole to make sure it was her and took a deep breath.

"Hi!" she sang out happily. "Oh man, I'm so ready to be done for the day."

"I bet you are," I said, grabbing my keys. "Let's go eat, and you can tell me all about your afternoon."

We got in my car and put on our seat belts. Before cranking the engine, I took a key from my key ring and slid it around and around until it was loose. I held the custom cut, tie-dyed key in the palm of my hand. It most definitely wasn't rainbow. It was tie-dye.

"I had this made for you," I said shyly. "In case you're ever in town and need a place to hang out instead of church. Or if I'm at work or in class, you could come take a nap or walk Keeper."

Allison took the key as if it truly were a gift. "I really appreciate this, Meredith. I will totally take you up on that."

Because of the serious stigma that key-giving often implied in sitcoms or chick flicks, I was inwardly worried about having made that move so abruptly. I didn't mean for it to be too personal or presumptuous, or imply that I was expecting anything in return. I merely wanted her to have a place to retreat when she was in town, to have someone she could rely on. I wanted to be that person. I had always wanted to be that person for someone.

She put the key immediately on her own key ring, and my heart smiled.

And so we made our way up the mountain to a local Thai restaurant that was surprisingly authentic for such a "sweet tea and biscuits" type of small town. It had quickly become a lovely, reminiscent way to enjoy the flavors I missed so much. Allison was a generous listener and so kindly allowed me to complement our dinner with stories from my time in southeast Asia. I showed her how Thais held their utensils, told her about the octopus food trucks, and my favorite papaya salad. Before I knew it, the waitress had brought our check. I still had half my food left on my plate.

"Wow, sorry if I've talked too much," I said, hurriedly scooping a few more spoonfuls of curry-soaked rice into my mouth.

"Don't be sorry!" Allison said and grabbed the black notebook. She slid her card in with the check and smiled.

"I've loved all your stories. Also, dinner's on me tonight since you bought my pizza and beer last time."

After boxing up my leftovers, we headed out to the car. The sky was so visible on the mountain, and the wispy clouds spackled a purplish shade across the sky. The sun was already beginning to set, and I was anticipating Allison having to head home soon.

As if reading my thoughts, she turned to me and asked, "So what movie do you want to watch?"

■ ■ ■

I blew on the DVD, rubbing off the smudges with my t-shirt. Allison had chosen her favorite (and rather lengthy) movie, *The Shawshank Redemption*. I had only seen it once, but I knew right away that the scathing themes, like judicial corruption and hope despite injustice, were right up her alley. As the opening credits began scrolling, I stood hesitantly by the lamp, wondering whether to turn it off. I hated lamp glare on the screen, and the television was giving off enough light to make it not too eerily dark. I made the executive decision, switched the lamp off, then was stumped again when I went to grab blankets. *Should I get one big blanket or two small blankets? The longer I stand here, the more suspicious I seem just staring at them. Just grab one.*

For nearly an hour, I managed to be completely engrossed in the movie. Allison and I talked periodically about important thematic issues or what mid-movie snack we wanted, but other than that, all was casual. Then, as

I scooted around to reposition myself on the couch, my foot came to rest against hers. My heart flickered a little, and I made the decision not to pull away. A minute, two minutes, three minutes went by and she left her foot there. I could've sworn she even moved it a bit closer. The rest of the movie was like a silent game of chess, move after move bringing us closer to a conclusion of the game we'd been playing. The prison warden had found the secret escape passageway, the action began to rise, and we were suddenly side-by-side. The movie was nearly over. I couldn't bear to lose the progress we'd made. So in one stealthy, slow, strategic move, I placed my head on her shoulder and held my breath. *This could be considered a platonic move, right?*

She moved closer, laying her head gently on mine, and that sealed the non-platonic deal.

Never had I ever been so elated to watch a fugitive crawl through a pipeline of shit.

The action began to fall, then the last scene of the movie began. I wasn't ready for the night to be over. As the credits rolled, we sat there, still.

"Wanna watch another movie?" Allison suggested quietly. Her voice was so close to my ear.

"Sure!" I said, jumping up and rummaging through my sparse DVD collection. "What would you like to watch?"

"Whatever you want," she said quickly and matter-of-factly.

We were definitely on the same page.

I popped in an old Judy Garland film, one of my favorites featuring Gene Kelly, then hopped back onto the couch where we fell effortlessly back to snuggling against one another. Allison commented vaguely on the opening musical act before reaching over to take my hand with a calm confidence. We interlaced fingers, and for the first time, I was home. Riding the wave of that adrenaline rush, I turned my head slightly to look at her. The television cast a subtle light along her mouth. Without a moment of hesitation, I kissed her, and she kissed me back. I wanted her to know, without words, how much I valued her. I wandered away from her lips, kissing her cheeks, nose, chin, forehead, and even the hollow of her eye. I could feel her face smile beneath mine. I held her face in my hands as if she were a precious and fragile thing. Slowly, she opened her eyes.

"I really, really like you," she said. Her eyes were glistening.

"I really, really like you too," I replied and held her close.

That was the first day of us. She stayed beside me and never left.

# 17

## COMING OUT

"It's the only way I know how to tell them," I said, gingerly folding the notebook papers and sliding them into an envelope. I'd written, revised, and rewritten the pages divulging my heart at least a dozen times.

"I support you in this," Allison said hugging me close, "and in everything. I just never expected you to tell them so soon. You know I don't *expect* this, right? You can take all the time you want."

"Of course," I replied.

We had only been dating for a single month when I knew it was time. I was too overcome with excitement not to tell the world I'd found my person, that I'd found *myself*. I was also weary of having to post vague captions on our photos or treat her like a buddy in public. Regardless of the outcome, I wanted to come out.

My family would have to be the first to know, and then I would work my way down a priority list of people until the trickling down of my honesty eventually spread to the general public. It was a stressful process even thinking of how to begin. I had barely given myself time to be whole-heartedly honest with myself, so planning a way to be honest with others was a daunting process. In an odd way, it was like thinking of who to invite to a party. There are, of course, the essentials. Family and closest friends are a given, but then there are those who skirt the "acquaintance line." Once you venture into that category, there's a ripple effect of "if I invite this person, then I have to invite this person," mentality, ultimately forcing the party-thrower to literally rank people based on their necessity. It's like a real-life MySpace. I found myself grappling with the same top-friends quandary, albeit on a whole new level of reality.

Relinquishing that responsibility of personal coming out conversations wasn't easy. But one day I came to a realization while talking to a mentor on the phone. She had been a friend of my family for decades, and everyone knew she was gay—happily partnered, even. Being among the few people I knew in the openly gay *and* Christian category, she was one of the first people I officially came out to. Showering me with love and congratulations, she also tried to prepare me for the hard road ahead. At the time, I didn't know just how hard it would truly be, but talking to her eased my mind greatly.

"Don't exasperate yourself telling everyone," she said. "Other people don't have to walk around announcing that they're straight! They don't have to have a sit-down, personal conversation and prepare themselves to the point of nausea just to be authentic."

I let out an audible sigh and almost laughed at how diligently I'd been trying to comfort and please everyone besides myself.

Without my asking, she offered, "And don't ever doubt the safety of your soul. It took me a while to be assured of that. God loves without condition. Remember that."

■ ■ ■

It was Easter Sunday when I told my parents. In hindsight, I wish I hadn't picked such an iconic religious day. The terrific amount of stress I held in my chest was brutal, but I clung to the symbolism of that day as one of renewal and promise.

I woke up that morning feeling hopeful. Allison's family was in town for the service, and I thought it would be a perfect time to have my family meet hers on oblivious and neutral ground. Perhaps their kindness would plant a seed that would weather the approaching storm. After a comforting embrace, Allison and I headed to church to play our separate roles. As I approached the church alone, I masked myself in the pretense that all was well. The service was beautiful and the sanctuary packed. We were a little late, so our family had to sit in the back row, where a line of folding metal chairs were set up for overflow. Unfortunately, this took Allison out of my view. My nerves were so jittery that it would've been nice just to have her in my line of sight.

I don't remember much about the service other than the fact that we all gathered in the garden for an egg hunt afterwards. There, my parents casually met Allison's family, and then we left for family lunch like a typical Sunday. Except that this wasn't a typical Sunday at all. The day was unceremonious and breezy compared to the anxiety I held inside. I sat at the table with my immediate family, grandparents, and cousin Karly, who'd driven in from out of town. The country buffet had us up and down, playing musical chairs and eating way too much banana pudding. We had stacked our silenced phones in the middle of the table so we could all concentrate on each other, but I would bet money that my focus was keenest that day. I soaked up every moment. From the material of my mom's shirt to the blackberry cobbler stains in the corners of Mamaw's mouth, I saw every detail. Perhaps it was an unconscious intuition that nothing would be carefree again for a very long time.

As my parents and grandparents paid the tab, I snagged my cousin in the parking lot. I was shaking as I spoke, and she was obviously concerned at my unease as I pulled the folded envelope from my wallet.

"Karly, I need you to do the most important favor anyone has ever done for me."

"Anything," she said. She had been among the first personal phone calls I made as I began coming out a few weeks previous, and her support was unwavering.

"I need you to give this to my parents."

The outside of the envelope read simply, *I love you.*

"Oh shit." Karly knew what it was. "Of course I will. I'm going to visit with them at their house for the afternoon, so I'll make sure I give it to them before I leave."

"I trust any way you want to handle it," I told her. "Even if it's throwing it and running." I tried to smile, but my face was tired and tense.

Karly hugged me close. "I'll text you when I've done it. You'll be okay."

I pulled out of the parking lot and started the long drive home, knowing I'd set the timer on a bomb that might destroy the thing I loved most in the world—my family.

# 18

## THE LETTER

In a huddled mess on the couch, I waited for the text from Karly.

"Why don't we do something or go somewhere to get your mind off everything," Allison suggested. "It's gonna drive you crazy just waiting like this."

I nodded and looked at my phone, which sat on the side table next to the couch.

"A friend of mine just got a job in California and is having a going away party in Birmingham. I'd love to see her." Then she paused a moment before saying, "I also think it would be safer for us not to be here."

I nodded again. It was truly a concern. I could just picture my mom coming to the door and demanding to talk. Whether or not it would be civil, I still just needed some space.

"I know you don't like these social situations with so many strangers, but I think it will be good for us to be away and for you to be preoccupied." Allison held me close and kissed my forehead.

"Let's go," I agreed.

When we arrived at the bar an hour later, I was still in a silent frenzy. Why had I not heard from Karly? My mind was conflicted between dwelling on my anxiety and concern about making a good impression on Allison's friends. I wanted nothing more than for them to see our chemistry, but my state of mind crippled my personality. There were over a dozen people, milling around tables with half-eaten hors d'oeuvres and chatting over their craft beers.

I smiled, genuinely happy to meet Mary, Allison's friend. The girl placed a flower chain necklace over my head and offered me a beer, which I politely declined. I stood to the side, grazing on a bowl of chocolate covered peanuts and watching Allison socialize, reminisce, take photos, and blow bubbles with the girls in the group.

Then my phone buzzed.

*I just left*, Karly's message read. *I told them to make sure and read the letter with an open and loving heart.*

My head whirled, thinking about how my parents were, at that very moment, reading my letter. The following minutes of silence had me wondering if somehow the bomb had been disassembled with reasonable understanding, or maybe just calm processing. I motioned for Allison, and she was beside me instantly. When I showed her the text, she immediately pulled Mary aside and explained the situation and the reason why we both seemed distracted.

"Why don't we take some shots together," the guest of honor suggested. "It'll calm your nerves *and* be celebratory! You came out today!" She was right, and I did appreciate her spirit.

"That doesn't sound like a bad idea," I relented. Trying to think of the least detestable option, I walked to the bar and pointed to the cinnamon whiskey. I got oil changes more frequently than I drank alcohol, so I figured that as long as I got it down, the effect would be near instantaneous. I tossed back one shot, then another, then another. Instead of feeling better, though, my head just felt like it was swimming through molasses. I wasn't so much calm as I was frustrated at the cloudiness that caused me to have to fight just to think. I *wanted* to think. I wanted to run through every possible scenario and assess my ability to handle it. Confronting the issue was inevitable.

I had barely slid my empty shot glasses back to the bartender when my phone started buzzing again, this time non-stop. My mom was calling. I showed the phone to Allison, as if I were a little child in need of someone to tell me what to do next. I sure as hell wasn't answering the phone. My screen shifted to a missed call banner, and I finally took a breath.

Then the texts came. And they didn't stop for months.

One after another, the texts built up until the number read 17. My eyes felt like a camera lens zooming away from reality, and I stood alone, poised to read the messages.

*Where are you? I'm outside your door.*
*Either answer me or come to the door.*
*You can't dodge me forever. Are you home?*
*It's not fair that you get to say what you want in a*
*letter and ignore me.*
*Meredith!!!!!!!!!!*
*Coward.*

I stopped reading, but they kept coming. I could not process the messages with all the alcohol in my system.

We left the loud atmosphere of the bar and walked the few blocks to Mary's apartment. I collapsed on the stranger's couch and buried my head in Allison's lap, sobbing audibly as the messages kept piling up. When I couldn't take hearing the buzz of incoming texts anymore, I squinted through the tears and silenced the phone. I tapped open the conversation just to erase the harassing number count, but not before I saw messages saying that I was a follower, a fake, a disgrace, disgusting.

Each one felt like my heart was being pummeled—yet, somehow, I was not the victim. I had been the one to damage things. I was the enemy. It was me. How silly of me to think my family would accept who I was.

I wept harder than I ever have. My body shook with the sobs, and I clung to Allison as if she were the only person left in the world. In a way, in that moment, she was. The world around me, the only world I'd ever known, the world I wanted to proudly show that I'd found the love of my life had disintegrated—but not before turning its back on me.

I could hear Allison crying softly too, and I will never forget that sound. Her tears weren't just sympathetic; they were a heart-wrenching, commiserating cry that made me ache even more. I had inadvertently dragged her into a painful tribulation. Coming out was supposed to be liberating and joyous, but my anxiety escalated with this new onslaught of horrible thoughts. I felt guilty for the pain this might bring Allison, I was frustrated by my family's outright refusal to accept it, and I cried because they might never see how truly happy I had become.

It was a contradictory mix of immense happiness and indignation. I was actually *angered* that my family couldn't see how happy I was. How counterintuitive. Perhaps, more specifically, it was how the situation was being handled. Like a child covering her ears and yelling in outright disregard for anyone else, my mom dismissed my reasoning altogether. The tears kept coming, but they brought more clarity with every drop. It was as if they were a detoxifying cleanse, healing my broken and confused heart.

As I remained crumpled in a pile on Allison's lap, I tried to put myself in my parents' shoes. Though a considerably difficult task, I attempted to adopt their "worst case" mindset and understand what they were going through. Like any parents, they had a preconceived, canned version of what they thought my life should be. I had already broken the mold by getting a BA in English rather than a safe, "it'll give you a real job" degree like nursing or teaching. Dating was never my thing, either. And not entirely because I questioned my sexuality. I was just a painfully contented introvert. The last straw, I suppose, was when I (while all my peers were having gender reveal parties for their second children) announced to the world that I was gay. My mom was mourning the loss of the future she wanted for me, while I, on the other hand, had to begin the long journey of accepting that her grieving process might not ever end.

I recently happened upon a blog post by a woman who attempted to answer ever-elusive questions about a broken relationship between a mother and daughter. My heart both sank and sang to read such a beautifully tragic rendition of my own life. The author described the relationship as a flowing river that sometimes reaches obstructions. Sometimes, as daughters who crave to please, we feel like the hindrance, the rocks in the stream. Because of *me*, a once smoothly flowing and happy relationship has become dammed. No matter how hard we try, though, there is nothing we can do to remove the hindrance. Why? Because the obstruction is not actually us. The obstructions are our silent battles: loss, embarrassment, spite, control, emotional instability, etc. We aren't responsible for moving blockages that are not ours to begin with. Not only are we not responsible, we are not *able*. I had to relinquish the obligation I felt to make everything right again. Maybe one day the boulder would be removed, but maybe it wouldn't. All I knew was that harboring such guilt would only drive me crazy and, in turn, make me an exasperating partner for Allison. I was my own river, flowing onward and hoping to converge with my mother again one day.

"Why don't you call in sick," Allison suggested. "You can't go to work in this condition."

I had not even noticed that it was nearly three in the morning. We had cried and clung to one another all night. Seeing the time finally shook me awake. I had to be at the gym for my 5 a.m. shift, and we were in a town an hour away from home. There was no way to call in sick at this point, even if I *was* sick. There was no one else to work my shift. My eyes throbbed as we gathered our things and headed out the door into the dawn. The drive was a blur, and the first few hours of my shift were a blur too. Although I didn't have anything the physician down the street could diagnose, I ached enough that it was evident on my emotion-torn face. Management sent me home, and for the next few days, I stayed snuggled on the couch next to my best friend. She was the only thing mending the gash in my heart between elation and utter heartbreak.

Here is the letter they received that day, every word exactly as I wrote it:

> *Marmee & Daddy,*
>
> *Please don't think that me approaching this matter with a letter is in anyway avoidant, insincere, or careless. As you know, I express myself better on paper, and a decision of this importance requires a clarity I know only writing can give. First, know how much I love you and how attentively I've sought your affirmation in my life. The reputation you've both helped me build and the validation you've given me throughout my life*

*are some things I'm grateful for on a daily basis—
so I hope you have enough faith in that sincerity
to trust that my realizations are not fabricated or
sudden. I am finally able to be honest with myself
regarding something I've known as long as I can
remember but haven't been brave enough to share. I
figured I would persevere through life attempting to
discover the feelings I am "supposed" to have, but
after years of searching, disappointment, and getting your hopes up, I am exasperated. I've worn a
mask for years, unknowingly succumbing to the bitterness and discrimination society has built against
same-sex relationships and convincing myself that
desires I suppressed couldn't be true. I've prayed every night for many years that God grant me peace,
clarity and direction regarding this feeling I have
that is truly rooted in the purest intention—not
lust, rebellion, lack of self-confidence, conformity,
or shock value as some might wish to assume. And
somehow, at this point in my letter, I feel as though
you're already upset with me or think that I've been
convinced of this "lifestyle" by social pressure—this
is by no means true. I've had these tendencies before I even knew them to be "wrong," and as I
grew up, I buried them further and further away,
vowing never to act on my desires unless something
providentially appointed gave me the reason and
wherewithal to be honest with myself—and therefore honest with others and you.*

*The night I signed up on that dating website again, a last effort to feign some false sentiment, I prayed—I prayed and begged God to give me guidance because I'd reached such a broken point. The next day, I met Allison—I knew from the moment I looked in her eyes that she would be my reason for coming out. The "you'll just know" feeling I assumed was a fairytale actually happened, and I know it was Spirit-driven. Unlike many who come out and are persecuted, I feel my relationship with Christ, the church, and Allison are all intertwined. I can't imagine that a loving God would create within me something that would later condemn me—a desire rooted in nothing more than love—nothing divisive or vile.*

*This isn't a confessional but a desperate plea for your acceptance. Granted, I know it won't be a seamless transition, so I will respect the time you need to process it all. Allison and I would be more than happy to talk with you about it later, but I thought it best to lay out my thoughts on paper first so there wouldn't be any irrational or emotional reactions anyone might regret.*

*I hope you can be excited for me because I'm happier than I've ever been. And despite the fear I've felt in preparing to share this with you, I am simultaneously elated. Allison has been so gracious through this process and will continue to be, but I want to protect her heart from any turmoil that* might arise. She is excited to be part of my life, and my family is that life. She is eager to be a part, but she understands the transition will take time. I just want, more than anything in this worldly life, for you to meet the person who fits me, gets me, cares for me, wants to grow alongside me. I want you to meet the person and see more than gender, to see a tangible replica of what I've had in mind for so long.

For the first time, I am secure in myself, so much so that I've taken this step to be vocal about it. Don't let close-minded people swindle the acceptance you can have for us. I'm not "back-sliding" or in-your-face, I just love who God led me to love. And I want you to be able to celebrate that with us void of worry. **Help protect me from those who will surely have unkind words to say.** Christ called us to love God and to love others. I'm more firm in my faith because I've finally seen how prayer, patience, soul-searching and seeking God's will has resulted in the desire of my heart.

I love you both with all my heart and soul. **Please love me through this.** I crave your love now more than ever.

"There is therefore now no condemnation for those who are in Christ Jesus..." Romans 8

Love,
Meredith

# 19

## MISMATCHED

I reached inside the front-load washing machine and grabbed the fin-shaped agitator. Like a turn on *Wheel-of Fortune*, I spun the rungs in search of straggling garments. There, wadded in the very back, was a reluctant sock—*her* sock. My heart warmed, as usual, at anything associated with her. It had been about a week since I'd come out to my parents, and we'd started doing our laundry together, a big step in my book. I remembered lamenting about all the unmatched socks, perplexed as to where the mates were, only to find out that Allison was an unapologetic sock mismatcher. There I was, eagerly trying to separate, search for, and reunite the lonely sock, but there were no matches to be found. Subtle, free-spirited qualities like these made me realize that having socks strewn around was okay. Life was messy, and the world already required so much structure. Why not let these little things remain in beautiful disarray? Perhaps it would help me make peace with the more paramount things that were out of my control.

As I bundled the damp clothes in my arms and walked toward the dryers, I became frustrated by the amount of time I was spending in the laundromat these days. God knew I couldn't go home to do laundry, so I tried to find contentment among the endless rows of whirling, swirling machines. I guess that was the root of my frustration. The *why* narrative of my laundromat trips was an ever-present reminder of being suddenly outcast. But I carried on and did my laundry with a smile because I truly *was* the happiest I had ever been. I dropped quarter after quarter into the slot and let the soothing clinks distract me from the time each coin was requiring from me—the dead space of time during the wash cycle when I waited and let that familiar worry creep over me.

I wondered if I would go to hell for loving her.

The machine and my stomach churned.

■ ■ ■

In the wake of my coming out, my mom fled to Florida to visit her sister. I guess it was to escape a reality she didn't want to face. In the meantime, though, I had the chance to go talk to my dad for the first time since it all happened. I had never, not once in my life, felt nervous to talk with my dad. His calm, patient personality had helped me maintain a sense of safety and consistency in an otherwise anxiety-laden adolescence. But for the first time, as I climbed the steps of our porch, I was terrified to confront the issue in conversation with him. I think my dad handled the whole thing pretty splendidly, really. Granted, it wasn't all unicorns and butterflies for him. My mom reiterated and reenacted his disappointment several times for me. That was to be expected. My dad's limited exposure to things unorthodox had him envisioning a life where I was taken care of by a man. Maybe it was just in his nurturing naiveté that he believed anything else to be unfathomable, uncomfortable, and just plain wrong. I remember the first time I spoke to him after it happened.

"I just want you to know…" his voice trailed off for a moment, "that I love you, and nothing can change that fact. You are my daughter, and I will defend you."

My eyes welled with tears as I was suddenly reminded of that classic children's book that he used to read to me. *I'll love you forever, I'll like you for always, As long as I'm living, My baby you'll be.* But then the conversation took a turn.

"But if you get married, I can't be there," he said abruptly. And that was all.

In one sentence, I heard how he felt. It said enough. The words hurt me deeply, but I received them graciously. I knew he didn't approve. I knew he couldn't bear to walk me down the aisle to anyone other than a strapping young man—to be "mismatched." I knew he loved me too much to say anything more. But that was just it—he *loved* me through it. What my dad did *differently* with the news as he processed it was what continued to set him apart throughout this process. He was the sturdy mediator between me and my mom during the heat of such a mess. I'm sure he got hell for it at home, but from that first conversation, he never let me go a moment unloved. Oddly enough, in some ways it made my dad and me closer. We talked more, and I prioritized him more than I ever had. I even began feeling guilty for having possibly neglected him (emotionally) as I was growing up. Being so focused on juggling my own misgivings, I often wondered if I had somehow forgotten to show him thanks for how much he had sacrificed. Did I make eye contact with him enough at dinner? Did I do things to make *him* proud, and not just my mom? Perhaps the solace I found, despite the shit storm around us, was that I was about to begin building a new and different relationship with my dad—hopefully one that would begin to facilitate a true acceptance for the real me.

# 20

## CHECKMATE

My heart beat fast and heavy as I walked later to meet my friend Peyton at the local coffee shop. Like a stone dropping into a swamp, every thud reverberated in my skull. She had warned me that I wouldn't like the conversation, and I spent each minute until our rendezvous wondering what that meant. Of course I knew she wouldn't approve, but I dreaded how she would approach the subject. My dear friend was about to splinter what little self-confidence I had built over the past few months. My ribs, like the fragile popsicle sticks of a child's art project, rose and fell with unsteady breathing as I sat down.

We engaged in meaningless small talk, I suppose as a means to warm ourselves up to the elephant in the room. Even if we hadn't planned on confronting the issue at hand, though, our conversation seemed forced, a thin fabrication of the comfort I'd once felt with her. Even before I'd met Allison, Peyton had seemed different and aloof.

Though her melancholic and emotionally elusive persona made her a hard nut to crack, she seemed to be real with me for the most part. We weren't best friends from the start by any means. The progression was akin to the stillness one would have to master in order to entice a baby deer from a shaded forest. I liked the challenge, though. And her friendship was truly worth it. Peyton was one of the most well-spoken individuals I had ever met. Our educational background was similar, and our hobbies and even our Baptist conversion stories were the same. That's why I ached as I sat down. I was about to lose a friend. I slid my wrought iron chair into the shade when we reached an awkward lull in the conversation. I knew she was about to state her case.

"I've been praying about this conversation for a long time," she began. "I'm going to tell you my thoughts on your recent decision, but feel free to tell me if I'm off-base."

Countering her argument was a feat I already didn't think I could handle. Her use of the word "decision" predicated her monologue with an unrelenting opinion, immediately killing any defense I might have prepared. The truth was, I didn't even *want* to argue. I was resolute in my "decision," but I also felt an unwavering and obligatory sense of compliance. She had helped me through so many emotional hurdles, and I truly honored her opinion. Why was it so hard to refute the people I loved? Instead, I willingly watched my character berated on so many occasions, merely because I didn't have the ovaries to woman-up and say, "Hey, your opinions aren't gospel!" Those people's opinions nowhere *near* reflected the truth and compassion of the Gospel, but it took a long while for me to realize that.

Peyton led with a hurtful truth. Like an infomercial therapist, she said my recent behavior stemmed from my mom. I couldn't deny that pleasing my parents and denying individuality—also known as filling a sink hole with irreplaceable fragments of myself—had drained me, and perhaps there was a void. Thus, Peyton gracefully yet cunningly trapped me in a vulnerable corner, making her first move in the systematic, theology chess match to come. The accuracy and sharp edges of her statement made me cry like a lonely child, and I sat still as she gave what she thought to be an orderly and rational account of my subsequent downfall into homosexuality.

Peyton ascertained that I was showing a lack of faith, had given up on men, and began clinging to girls. These had nothing to do with my being gay. And I think Peyton knew that. Even though it hurt at the time, I tried not only to defend myself, but I also tried to preserve my mother and her heart. Our issues were between us and God. I didn't appreciate the weak jabs Peyton took blaming my mom for it. It was bad enough that I was being perceived as a ruination, but now to also be seen as floundering and void of spiritual fulfillment—that was a nightmare. Apparently, I sought to fill this spiritual void with people. My series of friendships, some failed, some steadfast, were evidence of having sought earthly affirmation over the unconditional love and provision that only God could provide. Well-played.

I say this with hesitant sarcasm because although I believe spiritual assurance is necessary, I found it simultaneously absurd that my earthly relationships were being labeled as desperate attempts to patch my soul. Didn't God desire earthly creations to edify one another? The human race was created because God loved their interaction and their unified spirits that worshiped a Creator in one accord. God spoke specifically about not wanting creation to be lonely, yet me seeking stability from fellow believers was suddenly perceived as a shameful lack of faith. Then she twisted the dagger.

"I felt like I was becoming one of those people," Peyton said with conviction. "I felt like you were requiring more from me than I was willing to give, so I withdrew myself from our friendship. I felt like I was a disappointment to you, and as I desperately tried to keep up with your kindness, I realized I was just feeding an unhealthy relationship. You relied on me way too much."

I let the words sink in, then mentally retraced the past few months of our friendship. Unanswered text messages, her finding a new gym, new friends, no plans, only hellos. Here I was thinking I had apparently been a bad friend, and I was perplexed as to why she'd left. All along, I had just been *too good of a friend*. What did that even mean? I just wished I had known sooner. At the most pivotal and vulnerable point in my life, Peyton was nowhere to be found. I thought back to all the nice messages I had sent, the small, friendly gifts or random words of encouragement I gave to her, wanting nothing in return—just for someone to feel appreciated in ways I often didn't. I was embarrassed at the thought of having possibly been a burden, embarrassed that my kindness may have been seen as hopelessness, embarrassed that I'd opened myself up to the pain, embarrassed that I'd pushed someone away with *kindness*. How was that possible? She felt threatened or uncomfortable, and I was blind as to why.

Then Peyton gave me a diagnosis. She told me that I had "resorted" to Allison. Defensive indignation quelled the embarrassment for a moment as I realized that my love was being compared to a fleeting, sentimental fix or an illness needing a prescription. Allison was, according to Peyton's observation, next in the lineup of my serial friendships, and I had latched on to the first person who gave me the attention I wanted by succumbing to the weakness of same-sex attraction. Hurt, I narrowed my focus to suppressing tears. Intercepting the fiery darts thrown at my "spiritual emptiness" and my "weakness" regarding temptation were not subjects I was equipped to handle over a casual coffee meet-up. Those arguments would be better left for my book.

"You're not waiting on God's timing. You've just given up on guys because of your lack of confidence. You're not allowing God to direct your life."

These were all assumptions that, I'm sure, seemed applicable to those who were blindsided by my coming out. It looked like a rash decision because it was abrupt information, and it seemed as though I was making a declaration because the social climate was comfortable. I accepted the possibility of those accusations. But in fact, they were all *un*true. No one knew my heart. No one held my hair the night years ago when I vomited in nauseous confusion trying to figure out why I didn't want to be with guys. No one watched as the cogs in my mind whirled with thoughts of perpetual loneliness. No one helped ease my anxiety as I suppressed the feelings that spilled out of a closet I didn't even know I was in. In Peyton's defense, perhaps emptiness was a correct assessment. I *was* missing something. Unfortunately for her debate, my spirit was far from empty. It was brimming with a fervent, patient faith that God was leading me in the direction I needed to go—a direction guided by love, not temptation, and guarded from fear.

"Temptation, spawned by your emptiness, led you to choosing Allison. And *when* Allison is no longer enough to fill the void," Peyton projected, "you'll be doomed to embarrassment. You'll have to delete all evidence of her on social media, move away, maybe even change your name."

None of those suggestions were in jest. The person I loved was being compared to some kind of filler, like weak, plaster-filled holes in drywall that would crumble under the weight of a newly hung painting. I would have appreciated just one moment of benevolence, if only to acknowledge that on the other side of me was another human being with feelings. And not just any human, but *my* human. Even in the midst of vehement disagreement, I yearned for people to step back and see the loving person beside me not as a derision of their traditional ideals but as someone dear to me. Was I to be denied the luxury of love just because I fell into a category that some deemed unacceptable? I began to see the only agreement we and our naysayers would have, and that was agreement to disagree on the fact that my love for Allison was something pure.

"I can't help but feel that our friendship is somehow stronger and more honest," Peyton said without missing a beat.

I tried not to appear taken aback. Perhaps our friendship displayed honesty in those moments of conversation, albeit one-sided, but it sure as hell had not made us stronger.

"William is coming by in a minute to pick me up." Peyton stood, apparently satisfied with the conversation. "I'm gonna run inside and grab a latte for him. Want anything?"

I politely declined. Sliding the iron chair into a sliver of sunlight, I gathered my wits and tried to stop shaking. I wanted to leave. But I saw William walking from the parking lot, approaching too quickly for me to make a discreet exit. I had only met Peyton's new man-friend once. They'd met on a dating website, and I had no further opinion of him than if he were "Man #4" in the credits of a movie. And honestly, I felt he wasn't much more than that to her either. She, most times, seemed pretty uninterested in him. It wasn't my place to make a conjecture about her heart, though.

"How's it going?" said Man #4 in a voice indicating we were close friends.

I wanted to say, *Oh, fine, especially seeing as how I've been diagnosed with a condition deemed curable by a 12-step program*, but all I said was, "Fine."

We exchanged some customary banter, and I fidgeted, wondering how long it could possibly take to make a latte. Then, for some reason I can't even recall, the subject shifted to church, then some of Peyton's stubborn ideologies, and my ears perked up.

"She holds tight to that Presbyterian predestination dogma," William said, rolling his eyes in jest. "We had a big argument at dinner one night about our different opinions regarding man's free will and her Calvinist viewpoint."

"And?" I prompted.

"Well, she believes that God foreknew those whom He would elect and pursue for salvation. You know, Presbyterian doctrine. Man's depravity, election, limited atonement." His voice faded off as if to insinuate a *blah, blah, blah* type of emotion. "I, on the other hand, contrary to her stronghold opinion, believe we *choose* salvation. That debate could be never-ending, and supported and refuted a thousand different ways." William shrugged. "We will have to agree to disagree." He laughed. "She's pretty stubborn."

"Huh! How about that," I said in a sing-song voice. "Those pesky doctrinal disputes."

Peyton finally came back outside with William's drink. "I'm glad we could meet up and talk today!" she said with an air of finality.

"Me too, Peyton. Me too." I hugged her and knew it marked a definite change in the definition of our friendship.

Waving over my shoulder once more, I walked to my car, feeling satisfied. I'd been listening to someone who held fast to a dogma that had mankind's soul hanging in eternity's balance and wouldn't budge. How absurd and naive of me to think that she would understand. But perhaps she understood more than I knew. Something told me that when Peyton looked at me, she saw herself—and it terrified her.

■ ■ ■

About a year later, I saw William again. I was visiting a friend who was bartending a local restaurant when I saw him. I looked down the long, bustling bar, and there he was, sitting alone. As I approached him, I could tell he was a little intoxicated.

"Meredith!" he said, with more gusto than necessary. "It's so good to see you. Have a drink with me?"

"Hey William," I said, pulling up a chair. Us two (barely) acquaintances ordered a drink and a dessert to share.

"Just so you know, I never really had a problem with you and Allison. It's your own life. No one should interpret rules for you."

"Thanks, William, I appreciate that."

We sat there in silence for a moment sipping our drinks.

"It's my birthday," William blurted out. "She broke up with me on my birthday."

"Ohh." My brows furrowed in sympathy, but I didn't know what to say that would help.

"Peyton made a new friend at her gym." He knocked back a big portion of his drink. "The girl came to visit the other day, and I watched Peyton run to meet her with an embrace more passionate than any she'd ever given me."

That's all I needed to hear.

"It's not you, buddy." I put a friendly hand on his shoulder. "It's not your fault."

# 21

## WHEN THE COOKIE CRUMBLES

Several weeks after the debacle that was my coming out, I went to see a therapist. I had to spare Allison from any more of my rambling and tearful monologues. I didn't go to ask *why* I was gay, and I didn't ask my therapist to help me rationalize or justify anything either. I simply asked why I was facing such opposition and why the *hell* no one would listen to me. After a few sessions that were for the most part just a venting forum, I still had not cracked the code of why the anti-gay Christian community was rejecting me with such stalwart stubbornness—anger, even. The most definitive answer I got from that man with a menagerie of degrees was this: sometimes when we ask someone to question or explore even the tiniest part of their belief system, their whole cookie crumbles.

Growing up, I never questioned anything. Maybe it was in my nature, maybe it was because I had immense trust in my home environment, or maybe it was because I was afraid to. To my mind, the Noah's ark story *really* happened, mass genocide of the Native American population was *necessary* for colonization of the "greatest country on earth," and God banishes us to valleys of tribulation and sends hurricanes so we will learn to *trust*. Broad assumptions and embracing the traditional as fact was second nature to me—until my heart began to wonder. I knew, deeply and with purest intention, that I wanted to be forever partnered with a woman. But that desire came to a crashing halt at a wall—a wall binding and corralling me with all the things I had been taught were right and good. Solid family values stacked high and sealed by the mortar of unwavering southern heritage, good ol' boys, and subservience. We read the King James Version as infallible and denied teachings involving the phrase "millions of years ago." I never asked why. I just knew the Bible either told me so, or it didn't.

I soon and steadily began deflecting the lies that told me I was a depraved sinner. My mind, like the tip of an iceberg, was struck with enlightenment and began splintering into a deep intellectual chasm. It excited me. It *awakened* me. Some of the most intelligent (and faith-filled) people I knew cheered me on, championing my efforts to explore why I believe what I believe. I actually began to enjoy reading the Bible as if it were a real history book, supplementing it with commentary on the timeline of its authorship and the culture of the day. I stopped trying to rationalize the fairytale-esque events of the Old Testament and started to acknowledge that the writers' awe of God took a form beyond the capacity to be explained. I learned that fallible men wrote stories nearly a century after events occurred, and I shouldn't bank my salvation on whether or not we believe that Noah actually crammed all those animals on the ark, or if the earth was created in seven calendar days. These details are causing the types of divisions that cause churches to split and Christians to be hate-filled.

When these realizations hit me, I breathed a sigh of relief larger than I imagine my lungs could hold. I experienced a relief unlike any I had ever felt. The details, the "how it *really* happened," the misinterpretations, the contexts, and the arguments all began to dim. I began to see the Bible as a book, and God as a presence—not a wand-wielding magician in the sky. I began to relinquish the desire to know all the right answers because the people writing the Bible didn't have all the answers either. And we look to *them* for assurance? My priest gave a sermon once that described the Bible as a book answering the *why* not an exact manual showing *how* to do everything. Had I uttered such blasphemy within the walls of my Baptist church, I would have been banished faster than a gay person. To think that the ethereal presence of God could be contained in one book, written by imperfect men with no capacity or vocabulary to capture something so wondrous. And how disheartening to think that the same Presence that would write scripture with a holy finger would also stir seas, cause wars, and create cancer.

Christians often latch onto this detail, thinking that faith of that caliber *must* render them holy martyrs against any who dare confront them. Instead, it makes them fearful and cowering. Isn't fear a common theme in many evangelical circles today? Fear masked with anger. Fear masked with refusal to acknowledge that our world, our religion, even our God *moves*.

So many times, I have heard straight people in the Bible Belt mock the word homophobia saying, "we aren't scared of gays, we just think it's wrong!" Hysterical. But, in all actuality, phobia is an accurate term because many of us are too afraid to consider something outside of *our* normal—which often tends to be the only *right* normal in our eyes. Fear is often paraded about as righteous anger toward what "the left" is doing to Christianity. Crusading against historical and scientific facts which support the existence of a progressive religion, many Bible Belt Christians, myself included, have clung to "tradition" in order to justify aversion to the colorful, ever-changing swaths of our faith. How beautiful and, in fact, *welcomed* were many of the changes throughout history. Christianity was not meant to be a trailblazer to bring us up-and-coming cultural norms. It has *accompanied* changes while remaining the one, true, enduring thing that reaches out and over every shift that could ever come our way.

So, unlike those who fear to question the intricacies of our amazing faith, my cookie has not crumbled. It has remained intact and whole, perhaps even stronger—but would I be able to live out that conviction? Only time would tell.

# 22

## EMPOWER HOUR

The summer after we started dating, I got to see Allison in full youth-minister swing. Her beloved summer camp sessions were beginning, and not only did she recruit attendees from our church, but she also helped staff them (as she had done the half-dozen summers previous). Having not grown up going to any camps, spiritual or otherwise, I was a stranger to such large social gatherings. The only frame of reference I had was television shows where counselors blew bugles to wake everyone up, people paddled canoes all day, and kids found their boxers hung from flagpoles as a practical joke. Imagine my surprise when I joined Senior Camp mid-session and found myself surrounded by a large, cooperative group of respectful youth. There was song-singing, rallying choruses, and blessings chanted in unison. They were all extremely loud, and walking into the dining hall with more than one hundred cheering adolescents was sensory overload, but it was even more interesting to watch the transition from amped up energy to calm, introspective listeners.

Each day's program kicked off with a discussion of social issues and how we as citizens and Christians could handle them with more tolerance and grace. Taking into account Jesus's teachings and the baptismal covenant, campers learned to view current events through a religious lens. I was blown away by the fact that a church organization was talking about topics like war, race, sexuality, gender, science, privilege, and other politically charged themes. Not only did they discuss these topics, they revealed prejudices and considered all points of view. The only time such issues were discussed in my church growing up was when we mobilized and protested against any differing belief. I remember sitting in the pew before an invitational hymn listening to a deacon petition all church members to boycott Disney for advocating gay rights. My innocent mind couldn't see past the fear that I might not get to watch *Winnie the Pooh* anymore. And once a year, our church commissioned members to stand along the roadside to hold signs and shame those who'd had abortions. At the time, I thought it fun and brave to stand up for a belief. What I didn't stop to consider was the countless women driving by who were having to defend themselves against such accusations regarding their own body, decisions that may have saved their life, decisions they may have regretted. Were those of us out there standing on that roadside *really* pro-life?

Before breaking off into their small discussion groups, campers had the opportunity to make announcements about self-started activities that were available during free time. One day, a girl near the end of the hall raised her hand and was diplomatically recognized.

Having gotten the attention of all the campers, she said, "Today I will be leading an Empower Hour group to discuss LGBTQI+ issues. The meeting is open to those who identify as gay or for any allies wanting some insight. Even if you just want to listen, we would love to have you join us!"

Her announcement was met with a round of applause, and I sat speechless. A gay-themed meeting at a church camp that *wasn't* rehabilitation? I had to be part of that.

When free time rolled around, Allison and I made our way to a little arts and crafts cabin near the creek. I was stunned to see that around twenty high school kids had already arrived and were sitting in a welcoming circle on the carpet. I had previously told Allison that I wanted to be a silent bystander during the meeting; my coming out experience had left me so unsettled that just the thought of confronting the issue in any way still terrified me. My heart pounded so loud, I just knew everyone could hear it when we entered the quiet little room. After a few more stragglers made their way to the meeting, the girl who had made the announcement gave an introductory speech. In a mature and assertive voice, she requested that the meeting be a safe and confidential space in which everyone felt at liberty to speak without fear.

"Let's start by going around the room and introducing ourselves," the girl said. "If you would like, please also include how you identify or if you're just an ally listening in. By no means feel pressured, though."

My ears felt hot, and I dreaded the moment of hesitation before introductions began. If they decided to go counterclockwise, I was third in line to introduce myself. I didn't want that. I didn't want that at all. I hated traditional labels, heteronormative or otherwise. Once I labeled myself, I felt responsible for defending my answer. I breathed a sigh of relief when they began the introductions away from me. I looked sheepishly toward Allison. She smiled and squeezed my hand reassuringly.

As the campers began to speak, I was overwhelmed with gratitude that the upcoming generation felt comfortable identifying themselves as something unique. I also felt like a grandmother learning to use a smartphone. Terms like asexual, gender fluid, and intersex had my head spinning. It was no wonder there were so many new terms. Every person, whether they acknowledge it or not, has varying levels of how they identify with the gender they were assigned at birth. Some people experience no sexual attraction whatsoever, some drift between feelings of male and female mindsets, and some are even born with both genetic codes, thus both sets of reproductive organs. If that outward sign of genetic inner-workings is not enough to convince people of biological involvement in sexuality, I don't know what evidence will. Why would a loving God create something and then be angry about it?

As I listened to the introductions, I began to wonder about myself. I had been on dates with guys, but I had trouble finding them attractive. Was I bisexual in that case? I wasn't able to look at a societally deemed "hot" celebrity or a sexy stranger walking down the sidewalk and find them attractive in a romantic way because I had no *connection* with them. This, I learned, is called demisexual. So was that me? I did recall watching movies when I was younger and only being interested in the loveliness of the female leads. The whale trainer in *Free Willy* and Helen Hunt in *Twister* always had my full attention. I didn't know what that meant at the time. All I knew was that I was irrevocably in love with my Allison. If society labeled me a lesbian or what-have-you, then so be it, but I couldn't yet label what I felt. Frankly, I didn't want to.

"Hi I'm Allison, and I identify as bisexual." Allison took my hand and smiled. "And this is my girlfriend, Meredith." Her introduction was met with a chorus of *awwww* from the group. I peeked from beneath my visor. To be Allison's person was the only label I ever wanted.

When the introductions were over, I was surprised at the amount of diversity in the room that hadn't seemed to exist just twenty minutes prior. Some people had even voiced their sexual identities for the first time. I listened as the floor was opened to discussion ranging from the definition of all the LGBTQI+ categories to the campers' own personal experiences. An exceptionally outgoing young man, already out to family and friends, described the struggle at his school and how his car had been vandalized.

One girl wept over harbored fear as she wrestled with how to tell her sibling. Tissues went around the circle. Stories about acceptance, fear, self-loathing, and doctrinal beliefs vexed allies and gay members alike. There was such camaraderie in a meeting so voluntary. I was proud to be there, but also perplexed as to why I remained unbroken and dry-eyed.

Then, another camper spoke up and shared her coming out experience. I figured it would be like all the others. Contrary to what I'd imagined, the girl told a happy-ending story about how afraid she'd been before telling her family. Sick with nerves, she approached her mom with the news. Instead of causing the ruination of her family, the mom in the story simply hugged her daughter and said, "It doesn't matter, sweetheart. I love you just the way you are and support you no matter what." While this story was a salve to these heart-wrenching experiences, I desperately wanted that happy ending too. Suddenly, I was crying uncontrollably, pelted by every emotion, and pulling my visor down to hide my face. My heart ached with jealousy that I may never hear such beautiful words. Why me? Why did my current reality surpass every worst-case scenario I'd ever dared to imagine? As I wept, I became more aware of the pain I'd yet to confront, and that uncharted territory frightened me so much that I cried even more. And to top it off, I was totally embarrassed to have lost my shit in front of such stoic kids who were 10+ years my junior.

I was still hysterical when the hour wrapped up, and I dared not make eye contact with the campers because I felt so stupid. Instead, I buried my head in Allison's shoulder and walked quietly back toward our cabin.

"I'm proud of you," Allison said as the crowd dispersed. We were finally alone. "That was a ton of emotion and information to process in one setting. I hope you don't regret going?" Her tone sort of requested a response.

"No, no, not at all," I said, still choking a little on my weepy breaths.

"Hey, how about we go play basketball?" Allison suggested, changing our trajectory. She knew that was just the type of thing that would perk me up.

When we got to the covered basketball court, campers were swarming—some playing basketball, some groups dancing, and some hanging over the window of the snack bar grabbing cold drinks and candy. It was loud, but since I enjoyed playing, the frenzy was okay. As Allison and I stood in line waiting for our turn to shoot in the game, one of the boys from our youth group back home walked up.

"Sour Skittles?" Eli asked, offering us some of his candy.

"Sure," Allison replied. "Hey, are you bribing us with candy just so you can break line in front of us?"

"Nooo!" He smiled a sarcastic smile and proceeded to stay in front of us.

"I will take a candy bribe any day!" I said, taking a handful.

We stood silently for a moment as the line continued to move up. Then, with a small amount of hesitation, Eli asked, "Hey, why didn't I know you two were dating till today? How am I in your youth group and I *missed* that?"

"Surprise!" Allison said with bright eyes.

"I kinda figured," he said. "I had been rooting for you guys."

My heart warmed, suddenly feeling as if it had begun the long road to healing. I had already come so far.

# 23

## PARADIGM LOST

Those few days at camp prodded me along an agonizing mental evolution. Unlearning and relearning myself and my style of love as natural and not heretical wasn't something I could do overnight. My heart felt as if it were undergoing some sort of metamorphosis, painfully shedding an old way of feeling, which left me raw, but altogether new. My political shift took a similar turn after this realization—one that required me to allow sentiment *and* intellect to intersect.

Rewind to college when I was less than a week shy of my eighteenth birthday. George W. Bush was running for his second term. Despite the fact that I couldn't cast my vote, there was no mistaking where my loyalties were. I would've probably had a "W" sticker on my car if I'd had one, but a hat had to suffice. My political views at the time were canned versions of Fox News rhetoric, but I was proud of what I seemed to know. I was well-polished on all the hot-button issues, taking a polarized stance on things like gun control, abortion, the war on terrorism, and (oddly enough) gay marriage. My ideology was skewed, though, in regards to government involvement. *Dear Government, don't take guns or kill babies, but let's go kill all the bad guys, make the whole world a democracy, and tell people who they can marry.* That's about as deep as my opinions reached.

When I was a freshman in college I met a like-minded Republican named Zac. He was the patriotic type, the kind of guy who would voluntarily list the presidents in term order for the whole history class, thus asserting himself as professor's pet. We both loved our country. We loved talking current events and being the dark horses among liberal college faculty even more. Our parents warned us about those liberal professors, so we armed ourselves with a library of conservative materials. Zac and I even had a book-share program, complete with laminated library cards. We'd trade texts from Ann Coulter and Sean Hannity, scoffing at the silly liberals with every turning page. Tolerance and compassion were for the ineffectual and being a feminist was not at all Biblical.

Then I grew up. I can't spotlight one specific instance in my life that convinced me to veer away from right-wing extremism. All I can say is that it was a gradual, experiential awakening. I made friends with people who had vastly different life experiences than mine. I *did* listen to those pesky professors. I asked questions and challenged my belief systems. And then there was Thailand. Traveling was what truly unraveled who I was as a person, rebuilding me into a more insightful and appreciative human being. Living abroad and setting aside the privileged, conservative lens through which I viewed the world totally and radically changed my life. I saw families battling poverty and homelessness. I saw vast income inequality displayed in the education system where I worked. Some classrooms were equipped with smart boards, while others had rotting wooden desks and stray dogs on the floor. I experienced the upheaval of government corruption, and I feared the police and their puppetted loyalties to said government. I felt the loneliness of being a minority for the first time. I saw families working tirelessly, yet still living with thatched roofs and tattered clothing. When I was in Thailand, no one cared what denomination of Christianity I belonged to or what college football team I rooted for. In Thailand, I was viewed as a human, unedited and unaffected.

When I came home, however, I was injected back into a very privileged bubble, and I had a hard time readjusting. The global awareness I'd gained, along with the enlightenment of my education, was akin to putting on correctional lenses for color blindness. I began to see the dark shades of prejudice, glaring examples of racism, glistening elitism, and the contrast of inequality in all its forms—class, race, gender, sexuality, and any other divisive label. I began to listen to opinions from different cultures, news from different sources, and even ask myself some very harsh questions. Shielding myself with the Libertarian party for a while, I confronted very real and necessary issues, listening to my conscience rather than the rhetoric of the old south.

I began to see the confederate flag as racism, not an ode to heritage. I began to wear feminism proudly instead of casting it aside as a wildly inappropriate notion that women dare be paid as much as men. I began to see poverty as a twisted cycle, not a product of laziness. I began to see undocumented immigrants as hard-working refugees, not criminals stealing my job. Most of all, I began to see myself as a gay child of God, not a sinner in need of rehab.

I didn't just switch aisles, per se. Degrading my realizations to a mere party change on my voter registration card demeans the journey. It was more than that. The switch was an *awakening*. I began to ask questions, have doubts, look for answers, and seek out mentors. I would argue that I *found* my religion. In turn, I've adjusted my political views. There was a time when I viewed religion as a two-dimensional form, adorned with primary colors, moving in predictable, linear ways. Now I see it for the vast, dimensional, and vibrantly confusing concept it is. It wasn't until I understood the Bible as a sacred text rather than a scary rule book that I began to awaken my heart to its political guidance as well. Religion came alive and became more than just a heaven-versus-hell argument. The word "hell" actually isn't even mentioned in the Bible. Jesus referred to a physical place, a fiery garbage dump called Gehenna outside of Jerusalem, but not a place where we would be damned according to our works. Furthermore, while we are covering dicey topics, I believe that Jesus was the frontrunner of voluntary socialist principles. There, I said it.

Simply put, I am a progressive southerner pulling myself from the murky waters that birthed white supremacy and unrelenting prejudice, however unintended it may be. Have I left the South? Not yet, but I can't say it hasn't crossed my mind. I stay because I love the charm and resolve of my region. I stay because I don't want to desert a movement that I can herald as my generation's own. I want to be the change the South needs, and perhaps a representative for still-closeted gay Christians.

Zac and I lost touch for some years, but our paths eventually crossed again. Although glad to be reunited with him, I was wary of revealing my political shift. One day on the phone, as our conversation drifted to current events, the topic loomed, inevitable. Zac finally broke the ice.

"Hey, I want to apologize for being such an asshole in college."

"What do you mean?" I prodded, remembering him as a kind friend—nothing close to an asshole.

"Regarding politics," he stammered. "I don't know what your viewpoint is now, but I was an arrogant jerk back then. Life has shown me a lot, and I'm kind of embarrassed about how unfeeling and pretentious I was. I don't know about you, but I've left the Republican party behind."

"Really?!" I was ecstatic to have found someone who had experienced such a parallel journey, and completely separate from me, no less. I had friends who were existing conservatives and existing liberals, but it was comforting to know another intellectual who had made the journey across such the divide. I was so excited. "Well great, because guess what? I'm gay!"

"And you know what, Meredith? I am so, so happy for you."

Thus mine and Zac's friendship was revived from the ashes of a paradigm lost.

# 24

## INBOX

In the months after coming out publicly, I remember receiving counsel from another priest who offered these wonderful words of affirmation: "Meredith, you are not *going* to hell—you are *living* a hell."

And I was, truly. Texts continued to pile up in my inbox as the months went by. Allison begged me not to read them, but I did anyway. It was almost like a sickness. I desperately searched for the right wording, the right phrase, the most compliant answers that would make my mom listen to what I had to say—to have her accept me. But the thing was, she didn't *want* to listen at that point. She only wanted to remind me of her pain—a pain I wished every moment that I could take away, but it wasn't my responsibility. I received texts filled with pictures of myself accompanied by elegies and mourning. I was told to go off to a city where "my kind" dwelt then come back one day to apologize at the graves of my family members. She wanted me to choose between being in love and being with my family. My frightened, measly responses fell through the cracks of her own frantic and enraged logic. Exasperated and frightened, I eventually blocked them.

When *that* form of communication was thwarted, I started getting letters on my car. Some of them detailed why the Episcopal church (the church she once embraced) was the heretical stepchild of the Christian movement. Every line of the notebook papers were filled. When leaving them on my car was no longer a loud enough statement, she brought them to me while I was at work. There was no escaping the humiliation. Letters were filled with a type of bitterness and pain I don't even want to recount. Because deep in my soul I knew my mother didn't mean the things she said. Although they hurt me almost irreparably, the letters were able to be burned. The relationship with my mom remained amongst those ashes. I prayed that one day my mind would be cleansed of the wounds those letters had caused and be able to view my mother with limitless grace.

I still loved my mother—nothing could change that. And that's why it hurt so damn bad. I could not give up on her.

# 25

## I LOVE YOU, BUT...

Eventually, I was completely blocked from communication with my mom. All forms of contact on social media, text messaging, and calls were disabled. And so began the slow and painful attempt to slip away. My mom was mourning the loss of a daughter. I was mourning the loss of a family. Whether or not I found it to be nonsensical, the fact remained—the "old Meredith" was dead to her.

"Parents have these traditional futures in mind for their kids," a relative once explained. "I will be honest. I don't know how I would handle this if it were to happen to me, but you have *got* to understand, as difficult as it may be to see right now. Your mom loves you tremendously, but she's hurt beyond repair. I don't condone any of the nasty things she has said, but you realize she is grieving you, right? She wants the old Meredith or nothing, and I'm not sure if that will ever change."

It was eerie to think that I was being mourned. I felt like Tom Sawyer eavesdropping on his own funeral. But instead of that heartwarming feeling of being missed, I felt a frustrated indignation. I wanted to jump into the middle of her ceremonious grieving and shout, "I'm here! I am alive! I'm still me!" The awful part, I guess, was that the new me wasn't welcome, and there was nothing I could do to change that. So I continued to watch the suffering as a guilt-ridden bystander, chained in the attic above my own funeral. Even though I disagreed (with utmost vehemence) that the "old me" was gone, I couldn't deny that the white picket-fence, heteronormative, snow-globe future my mom had envisioned *was*, in fact, dead. My only hope was that one day she would want to meet me and get to know me again. The same me.

Before going completely dark, my mom told me that many of my friends at the gym had come to her in solidarity, reassuring her that I would "be back" and that my "lifestyle was just a result of low self-esteem." I stopped reading and began to wonder who these people were who'd been playing both sides of the fence, feigning support and simultaneously soothing my mother. I was embarrassed once again that I had been falsely labeled as having low self-esteem. Why must there always be an excuse as to why someone is gay? I was also deeply offended that my beautiful relationship had been compared to a dark alley down which no one else dared travel. I would "be back"? Be back to see the pious people keeping vigil at the gateway of my "lifestyle"? Be back because I was so immature as to make a commitment to someone and cast her off like last year's fad? Be back with newfound self-worth because of all the encouraging comments I'd heard from them along the way? Be back to be lavished with conditional love? Thanks, but no thanks.

As if this betrayal alone wasn't hurtful enough, I still received periodic emails. Against Allison's gentle suggestion and more steadied judgment, I read each and every one with hopes that she would reach out with a desire for a reconciliation. I held on to those hopes until the day I received one with the subject line "FWD: lesbian child."

In the email was a conversation between my mom and radically conservative radio talk show hosts Rick and Bubba. I had never felt so exposed, so embarrassed, and so alone. Reading their conversation felt like walls collapsing around me, suffocating my attempts to make sense of why she would do such a thing. Rick and Bubba (their show a nationally syndicated broadcast airing on 50 stations spanning 15 states) are household names in the south. My mother's initial email to them was sincere, and honestly more love-filled than anything I had witnessed in months. She told them I was the most sound-minded Christian she knew, that I was honest, full of discernment, and that our relationship was unmatched by most mother/daughter duos. Just those few sentences helped to mend my wounds. Then she did something incredible. She asked them about my eternity. Two radical radio hosts were given the chance to give their opinion on my eternity. Not a counselor, not clergy, not family, not research or study, but Rick and

Bubba. It was now obvious that she was crying out to any moral compass she could find that would listen and feed her back the words she wanted to hear and believe.

Rick responded in an authoritative and pompous manner, telling my mother about a local intern who had struggled with same-sex attraction. They had advised him to either suppress the feelings and remain single (against his desire), or marry conventionally and pray to be instilled with the desire to create a heterosexual, nuclear family. I was speechless. Delving into theology would be akin to opening Pandora's box, and that's not the purpose of my story. Rick and Bubba, in their "righteous" interpretation of scripture, wanted to deny their intern the goodness of a relationship he wanted. They wanted to prevent him from hearing and feeling (from a partner) the most beautiful grouping of words in the human language: I love you. They wanted him to feign affection and possibly bring children into a marriage that would surely crumble. They wanted to define love for themselves, not let it be unconditional, real, and true. Then, at the end of the email, Rick signed off with, *Pray, pray, pray that the Lord reveals His authority to her and she submits to Him totally. She needs to love Christ more than her sexuality.*

This incident left me reeling in anger. How dare they further indoctrinate my dear, vulnerable, and hurting mother before I even had the chance to tell her about my heart. Yes, they were entitled to their own opinion, just as I was entitled to make my own opinions known. But where I was listening and trying my best to respect such condemning views, wanting to adopt the same open-mindedness that had helped me accept who I was, they could not even begin to reciprocate. Instead, I was cast off by these men as a child laden with a "sickness" that I had control of curing.

"I would rather be hated than tolerated," I told Allison one day.

It was true. I could withstand hatefulness better than the consoling statements that inevitably began with "I love you, but..." Hate is just fear in disguise. Hate often clings to tradition, sadly ending up on the wrong side of history. Hate can be eradicated, but it is arrogance that breeds the dreaded "I love you, but..." The admonition then becomes the main event. The empty sentiment at the beginning only softens the blow, making its speaker seem as if they're being constructive and compassionate. What they *really* mean is that authority on any subject is decided by them, and we are loved *despite* our disparaging ways. When hurtful words follow "I love you, but...," I am more and more desensitized to how holy and wonderful those preceding words truly are.

Did that radio talkshow host realize how hurtful he was being? Or was I just a two-dimensional problem on his computer screen? I wondered if there was anything that might allow Rick to reevaluate his viewpoint, reconsider narrow ideas, and approach the situation with more compassion. What if I were his daughter? How prophetic my musings soon came to be.

# 26

## I'LL MEET YOU THERE

When I departed Thailand, my flight left Bangkok before dawn. I was fortunate enough to be connected with a beautiful family in the city who hosted my final evening. The family lived together in a large, modern home—a far cry from the more rudimentary living I'd experienced up north in the mountains. The daughter, Oui, lived with her parents and husband, all of them bankers or well-to-do flight attendants for a Thai airline. In the small amount of time I spent with Oui, I couldn't help feeling the true love and kindness that radiated from her every action. Having worked with the airlines for quite a while, Oui's English was solid. Her face was flawless and her style, effortless.

Before bed that last evening, she brought me a pizza from a recognizable chain restaurant. In contrast to the isolated town where I had been, Bangkok was an international hub filled with things with which I was familiar. Oui beamed with pride as she delivered what she considered to be true "American cuisine," the thing I must be craving after this whole year away. Though I would've never deflated her excitement by telling her, I would have actually been happier with a culturally rich last meal. But I couldn't dispute her attentiveness. After putting the pizza beside me, she reached into her pocket and pulled out a colorful, beaded necklace with golden clasps.

"I have this gift for you," she said, cupping the necklace lovingly in my hand. Thais were unfailingly affectionate. "I want you to always remember Thailand."

The colorful array of beads rolled around my hand as I examined it and let her see the joy spread over my face. She hugged me goodnight and retreated to what I thought was a closet alongside my guest room. She emerged maybe fifteen minutes later. I waved a final goodnight, my mouth full of pizza. A fragrant smoke trailed behind her, and I waited for her steps to disappear down the hall before examining the room where she had been. The tiny compartment was a prayer closet. I could see a shimmering statue of Buddha through the darkness and smoke. The Thai Buddha, thinner than the more widely known laughing, fat Buddha of China, represents a different school of thought called Theravada Buddhism. It was fascinating to learn about. My family feared that my interest was an imminent path to conversion, and I spent many a conversation reassuring them that my interest was simply respect and not a reconstruction of my faith. Oui's prayer closet had a birdhouse-sized temple atop an ornate pedestal. As was tradition in most practicing homes, food and gifts were placed on the tiny temple thresholds. Sodas and plates of food equipped with forks and straws decorated the platform. It made me chuckle to imagine Buddha drinking pineapple Fanta from a bendy straw.

It was on this night that I reconciled the stark religious contrast and simplified such theological differences into a single, inclusive concept. Faith, at its core, takes its seeker on a journey to obtain ultimate safety and peace in the arms of the Creator. My path is through Christianity, substantiated by the gospel and propelled by the grace and everlasting love of a Savior I call Jesus. I believe in a Maker of all things, seen and unseen. My lack of understanding regarding other religions hovers in that "unseen" realm that I can't fathom. How arrogant of me to think that I could uncover the validity of every person's journey. I believe in my one way, truth, and life, but I will never call another faith-led person wrong—just as I would be upset to hear someone defame *my* faith. Consider the kaleidoscopic array of denominations there are just within Christianity. Each doctrinal interpretation is different, and perhaps in a passive-aggressive way, each ambassador of each new sect felt others to be intrinsically wrong, thus breaking away and creating even deeper division. Modern crusades of militantly evangelized faith are so toxic. We simply *aren't* God, and how dare we try to be.

Theologian and member of the United Methodist church, Rev. Roger Mosely wrote in his book *Kissing Fish* that "each of the major world religions are like wells, and if you go deep enough into any of them, you'll hit the same aquifer and Source." He goes on to say, "I firmly believe that. However, I'm particularly drawn to the well of Christianity." Roger even cites the infamous verse in John's gospel declaring that no one comes to God without first going through Jesus. Roger explains this, in his spiritual opinion, as a verse "celebrating the uniqueness and distinctiveness of Jesus and also celebrating the universal common ground that exists among many religions." We follow Jesus, but we mostly follow His *ways*. "All those who follow Jesus' way, teachings, and examples," Roger explains, "—the way of unconditional love, of radical hospitality, of loving-kindness, of compassion, of mercy, of prophetic speaking truth to power, the way of forgiveness, of reconciliation, and the pursuit of restorative justice—by whatever name, and even if they've never even heard of Jesus, are fellow brothers & sisters in Christ and His Way."

I could never look Oui in the eye and say, "You're wrong." I simply could not. I could never say, "You're going to hell if you don't change," when, in fact, I wasn't even sure if hell even truly existed. In one flippant phrase, I would have essentially condemned half a billion people. If that isn't arrogance, I won't live to ever understand it. Telling someone they are misguided is assuming every strand of a person's morality and ideals to be identical. We all have differing belief systems. Storing such critical energy toward others who are different then makes religion nonsensical. Collecting bits of rage along what should be a path to one's own perfect peace seems remarkably stupid. This type of judgment stems from a burning desire to change someone else into a clone of one's own intricate and unique tower of ideals. In an article written by relationship specialist Carolyn Hidalgo, this conflict can only subside with the realization that we are not everyone's spiritual compass. Hidalgo says that, "doing this does not mean we accept or absolve responsibility for all manner of words and behavior. It just means that we stop blaming and judging someone else and consider that they're doing their best from their own state of consciousness."

So I respectfully stand in my arena of Christianity and play by my own rules. I can't referee a basketball game and throw a flag for pass interference. That penalty only applies to football. A basketball game would go nowhere if other rules applied, and so will our relationship with others. We get nowhere if we impose ourselves on something as sacred as principle.

Narrowing the focus and applying this within my own religion (and the distinctive denominations within it), I saw the necessity in complete surrender. For the first year of my relationship with Allison, I held tightly to the obligation of defending our relationship at a Biblical level. I had read articles, sought council from ministers, studied word origins and culture, but still found no peace. I could eloquently give combative opinions on each of the six verses in the Bible seeming to condemn homosexuality. I welcomed the conflict, almost craved it. I wanted to impress someone with what I knew and make them think twice about confronting a gay Christian with the Sodom and Gomorrah story ever again. But honestly, what was there to prove? Why did I feel so defensive? Anything I said, even if it were a signed and sealed epiphany from God Himself (or Herself), would not have caused the belief systems of naysayers to cave. In a weird way, I kind of commended the strength of conviction in those who wanted to persecute me, even if their conviction was rooted in ignorance. If only I could've been unwavering like that.

Then it hit me. Allison never seemed worried about looming theological debates, Greco-Roman contexts, or any of the thesis-length conclusions I'd come to. Granted, these studies were good for my research-loving, plan-focused mind, but after the dust of my inner frenzy settled, there sat a person who was just as confused as ever. And then there was Allison—a person whose ethics I thought to be more solid than anyone I knew. Allison didn't need to hand out pamphlets, or frankly, write a book. She only said, "You know, there's a quotation by the poet Rumi I really love."

*Beyond our ideas of right-doing and wrong-doing,
there is a field. I'll meet you there. When the soul
lies down in that grass, the world is too full to talk
about.*

# 27

# NAYSAYERS & YEA-SAYERS

Being gay immediately pegged me as an activist with an agenda. I've actually never had any agenda other than to be happy and try to make other humans along the way happier too, so I continue to be frustrated by this rhetoric. An "agenda" happened when I was inundated with hurtful words and forced to build a defense beyond *just let me be happy*. Instead of remaining in the line of opinionated fire, though, I decided to crusade for those too hurt to lend their voices to acceptance's cry.

Of course, within a year of my coming out in early 2015, LGBT issues headlined both the church and the nation's newsreel. The climate of my timing seemed a perfect storm, but sometimes it was just a plain ol' storm. I remember the day gay marriage was legalized nationwide. I was at work when the decision was announced. I casually picked up the remote and turned the lobby television from the weather channel to the news channel. The headlines were profound, and the live, celebratory shots of supporters around the country were enough to make my eyes sting with happy tears. I snuck my phone from the drawer, ran to the bathroom, and texted Allison a line of multicolored hearts.

Happiness was quickly undone as, throughout the day, my social media newsfeed became littered with evil-purging articles and gnashing of teeth. My strength to withstand that type of controversy was nowhere near Allison's, so I moped around, weeding through the bitter articles to the more uplifting ones.

"How about we celebrate today with some frozen yogurt," Allison suggested.

I quickly agreed. Detaching myself from the negative newsfeed was a smart idea, and one I think Allison strategically planned.

We were like kids in a candy store as we went back and forth between colorful yogurt handles and toppings. Our goal was to make the most colorful dessert to commemorate the day, then surprise each other with the result. I covered the bottom of my bowl with a smooth, cake flavored yogurt and delicately placed some colorful candy on top in a rainbow arc. We hid our yogurt cups until we sat down, then I peeked over into Allison's bowl. Hers was a lot more robust, to say the least. Tiny, swirling peaks of multi-colored yogurt filled the bowl, candy and fruit with corresponding colors piled on top. There was green apple, red velvet, orange zest, and all the rest of the rainbow colors. We laughed and took photos until her yogurt began to melt into a muddy mix of interesting flavor combos.

The commotion lasted well over a week. Newspaper, radio, and talk-show hosts latched onto the issue, stoking controversy. A day or two after the decision, I noticed rainbow and equality symbol overlays covering social media photos of LGBT couples and allies alike. It was encouraging to see people from my community and church and even allied heterosexual couples voicing their support. Within hours, conservative Christians retaliated. Covering their photos was an image mimicking the style and color scheme of the equality symbol, but with the parallel lines made into a cross. It made me angry to see a symbol from my belief system become the counterargument to love. That moment proved a major crossroads for me.

Several months prior to meeting Allison, I had watched a friend journey through a coming out process that would prove similar to my own. I watched and listened to her struggles as the conservative Christian family to which she belonged slowly ostracized her with fiery passages and hateful opinions. In the wake of that disastrous reaction, her faith was left behind in a bitter and pitiful retreat from all things religious. In trying to beat their fundamentalist opinions into her head, the family unknowingly beat her spirit past a point of no return. My friend, still a symbol of heroism to me, has since dissolved her relationship with many members of her family as well as her relationship with a God she found unmerciful. Do I blame her? No. Do I weep for her? Yes. Because it was not God who called her an unworthy member of the Body, but God's representatives on earth who did—people supposedly equipped to be a loving force for the Kingdom.

When I found myself at the very same crossroads, feeling mocked by the very Christians I associated myself with, I suddenly had no desire to share their label. I wanted to run away saying, *Look what those Christians are doing! Does anyone else see their close-minded heresy? Why would you want to be in communion with them? Won't they listen to my opinion for just one second?* My defensive anger let me consider a life of apathy, but I couldn't. I had Allison, who embodied all things opposite of apathy. Her approach to life, social issues, and spirituality was so robust. If I fell into a shadowed, bitter hole, it would have only hurt our relationship. So in that moment, I decided to clothe myself with the Gospel and pour all of my negative energy into a much quieter task—the process of transforming angst into a project of patience. And so I started writing.

I treated my journey like one intensive research project, complete with interviews, documentaries, counseling sessions, and scholarly articles serving as my sources. Life itself was my main source. Whenever I reached a glitch in my study of God's love or Old Testament history, I would stop and ask myself some basic questions:

> *Is what I'm feeling compelled by love, not infatuation? Yes.*
> *Is what I'm feeling unmarred by obsession or vice, thus pure? Yes.*

*Is this love a specific answer to prayer? Yes.*
*Is the love I feel real and steadfast? Yes. A thou-*
*sand times, yes.*

There were, and I anticipate there to still be, pitfalls of doubt along the way, but is that not true of any journey? My first six months of being out publicly were particularly hard. But it seemed that on the rough days—whether hatred was blasted from media, friends, or family—I would have something equally calming.

I was fortunate enough to meet and be ministered to by a wonderful soul during those first stormy months. I met Sharon at a young adult camp session one blissful, restful weekend as she guided the group through meditative prayer and active resting. Being the priest in charge of the program, this guardian angel of sorts helped calm my anxious mind. One day, she led a small group through the labyrinth in a nearby garden. When asked to give a definition for the term "labyrinth," I first thought of a confusing hall of mirrors at one of those abandoned parking lot carnivals, or an intricate maze for white mice in a science lab. It wasn't until I walked the path of a prayer labyrinth that I gleaned a whole new meaning, something altogether different.

Sabbath was the theme of the weekend. We were learning how to detach our souls from busy life, be still, and know God. I felt slightly impious for not knowing how to properly engage in a sabbath beyond attending a church service and taking a nap. I'd been going to church since gestation, so why was this so new? Intrigued, I followed Sharon and a few others up the road to where a small wooden sign etched with the word "labyrinth" pointed into a patch of woods. It was the only indication that anything beyond pine trees and armadillos existed in the direction the tilted arrow suggested.

In its simplest form, aesthetically speaking, a labyrinth is a pathway in which the entrance and exit are the same portal. The path covers a quarter of the circular design, folding back onto itself as it reaches the center. Then, unexpectedly, the path drifts outward again into another quadrant, taking its journeyer further away from any apparent progress. The pace is winding and confusing at first, so the small circular hub of the labyrinth feels like a safe haven. Following the path once more (going backwards), the journeyer eventually finds the end.

Oh, the symbolism. I was enthralled as Sharon compared the prayerful walk to our Christian journey. No visual and experiential moment has ever brought such clarity. I was at a point in my life where I was doubting my spiritual walk and discounting it as unholy, yet in that moment, God was inviting me to continue. The winding pathways were life's journey, with the destination being the heart of God in the center. We walked symbolically through segments of our lives, drawing closer to God, but we could, in an instant, be set back by circumstances of staggering doubt or problems that wished to ensnare. Sharon suggested we meditate on a certain prayer or thought as we walked. Unprepared for such an inward journey, I took small steps and just quieted my mind. I saw obstacles in the brush, became confused when turns were unclear, and battled my mind's desire to be distracted by passers-by. I needed guidance, and the only applicable passage that came to mind was Psalm 23. Quoting it over and over again, I traced the lines as intricately as I traced my path through the labyrinth and ultimately to God.

When I got to the third verse, "He leadeth me in the paths of righteousness for His name's sake," I heard a different version than I'd ever heard before. As a Christian, I had submitted myself to God, therefore I had submitted myself to a life of fearless pursuit. Once begun, there was no turning back. Intricate and irregular as the path might have seemed, also indicative of my own journey, the desire to press on drew me closer to God once again. Righteousness is rooted in love, and as simple as it might be, I had lost sight of that promise. The trials in my life had shaken my confidence, and I wavered in my faith, but sanctification was a cleansing gift. The labyrinth taught me that although our lives are intricately unique, our path is as simple as submission and steadfastness—even in our darkest hours.

Later that evening, my last night at camp, I approached Sharon with the burden that I'd carried throughout the labyrinth. I have always been fearful of approaching strangers with anything personal. Listening is my best form of communication. Nevertheless, I felt compelled by her crusading spirit, and it somehow made me brave. I knew early on that she was an openly gay and partnered member of clergy, so I knew I could glean some insight on how to handle my weary mind. A mere request for prayer soon became follow-up phone calls, dinner discussions, and uplifting text messages that always seemed to appear the second I needed them—messages reminding me of God's unconditional love and my worth. They bombarded my heart with peace like a soothing balm.

"I have a few years rooted in the Baptist church too," Sharon told me. "It made me doctrinally sound, but it also made me understand fully how hurtful the fundamentalist version of the denomination can be. Embrace God's peace," she urged me more than once. "Perhaps time will heal your mother. Then again, maybe it won't. And that's when you'll need God's peace the most."

I held tight to her words, read the books and articles she suggested, and remained in a constant state of prayer. But I received ridicule. My efforts at studying the language and contexts of the Bible were mocked. My efforts to pray about the health of my loving relationship were called blasphemous. That was a hard pill to swallow and sent me to a dark place of doubt many, many times. I was relentlessly accused of searching only for the information that would justify my "sin," and for only seeking counsel from people who were gay. I was on a mission to battle the *premise* of that accusation by proclaiming that the definition of true sin is one that leads its vessel into destruction. Biblical texts *do* showcase sinful, subversive behavior, but it is *always* predicated by a need to defy God's will, and it *always* results in a domino-effect of ruination. Besides the stones of persecution being hurled from all sides, nothing about my love for Allison was destructive. Contrary to the accusations, I simply wanted to unlearn misinterpretations and seek what the Gospel expected of me. In doing that, I felt more and more welcomed as a member in not only the Christian community, but in the Body— one in which Christ arranged and rejoiced that every different and *unique* member was honored.

Allison and I had been together nearly a year before I truly began to believe that I was loved by God. For so many years, I feared God—and I don't mean the respectful and reverent type of fear. I was utterly terrified of the Being lurking around me who would send bolts of lightning to strike down my every unchaste thought. I walked gingerly on earth, terrified by the fiery red demon below who was seeking to ensnare my every step. I later came to view God as a creator who was loving, as a benevolent Being who might actually be cheering us on, championing us to love others. What a pleasant thought. In turn, I became more and more comfortable with how I was created. Sure, I had been able to counter those who called my relationship a choice, but those who said I needed to resist the "sin" proved more difficult. I had yet to embrace a steadfast bravery.

# 28

## LET YOUR HEART BE LIGHT

That bravery waxed and waned. Most times, my confidence depended on my surroundings. At church, I felt safe. With a handful of affirming friends, I felt genuinely loved. Outside that very small community, though, I was frightened. Our landlord was very skeptical of mine and Allison's relationship, several times questioning if we were just *friends*. What if we were kicked out of our apartment? That's still legal in Alabama. Anytime we went to buy groceries, I canvassed the parking lot first. What if we ran into a family member? I caught my breath around the turn of each aisle, praying I wouldn't have to face a confrontation or subject Allison to any public ridicule. Eventually, we started shopping in the next town over. I watched as my family bickered over politics and sat tolerantly by as they heckled me for attending a Bernie Sanders rally. Branching off from our "conservative family values" suddenly made me the hippie liberal misfit. For a while, I felt cast aside.

But honestly, that *aside* became a space for me to recover and perhaps a space where my mom could, too. Instead of recover, though, I think she entered a phase of denial which, unfortunately, masked itself in compliance and mild understanding. And that was the only way we were able to make it through our first Christmas as a broken family.

Although it would be an unequal sacrifice, I was willing to try and make peace for our Christmas together (completely eliminating my new life from conversation), if only the yelling would stop. As Christmas drew closer and closer, though, I began to wonder what my holiday would actually look like. I was conflicted because I *wanted* to celebrate with my family, but I was also upset knowing that Allison couldn't be involved. Again, the compromise was excruciating. To be completely honest, what I *really* wanted was to begin our *own* tradition, void of guilt or obligation or compromise—just us, the family I wanted to build with her. But things were still too new. I would either have to make a slow and graceful exit from my own family holidays, clinging to a hope that one day Allison would be welcome, or I would keep going and be eternally "single" while my family members and their significant others got to feel the warmth of togetherness.

I would have to take it one holiday at a time.

And so, it was only a week before Christmas when I got a text from my dad asking if I wanted to spend the holidays in New York City. All twenty-eight of my past Christmases had been spent at home with coordinated pajamas, breakfast casserole, and nostalgic Rat Pack music playing in the background. I couldn't believe that our tradition was about to be broken, but who would turn down such a magical opportunity, a once-in-a-lifetime trip? Not to mention, this 90s kid wanted nothing more than to see the setting of *Home Alone: Lost in New York* in real life. The Plaza Hotel limo scene with the steaming pizza, the Rockefeller tree reunion with Kevin's mom, and the pigeon lady in Central Park were iconic scenes of my childhood. I immediately arranged my work schedule and sent an affirmative reply full of all the festive emojis I could find. Vacations were always a big deal in my family. My dad has always been the best at planning family outings and making sure our time is filled to the brim with learning, adventure, and good food. He spares no expense, monetarily *or* emotionally. He lives every day to be the best father he can be, and not even my coming out as gay could cause him to change that.

My family was not the beach type. The thought of going to a hot, sandy beach to sit, get burned, read a book, and play in shark-infested waters was not one my family entertained. An evening spent at the overrated seafood restaurant, overpriced mini-golf, or overdone matching-outfit photos were not enticing either. My dad was the type to have printed itineraries for each family member, tours already booked, and restaurant reservations set. We braved an already-planned trip to Washington, DC, a mere two weeks after the attacks on September 11th. We drove across states, playing road trip bingo and testing our family harmony skills with opera-style karaoke. We explored Nova Scotia to its fullest, watching whales and staying in adorable cottages along the way. I wondered how this trip to New York would compare to this series of sweet memories.

What I failed to realize was the hefty stipulation involved in this new era of my family's vacation dynamic. The bargain, although not officially stated, was not an easy one. I joined my family vacation knowing that I had to hide the most vibrant part of my life, and that was Allison. It went beyond just the frustration of having to pretend to be single again; It was an ache that lurked around every corner. I was mindful of my pronouns, never mentioning "we." I had to reroute topics of conversation when they began leading back to Allison. I couldn't simply walk by a store and say, "Allison would love that." I bought some souvenirs for myself, but they were really for her. When I passed by her favorite shades of blue, I held my tongue.

My parents picked me up on Christmas Eve before dawn so we could catch an early flight. Allison woke up with me and helped to get my luggage downstairs. I cracked open the front door to let them know I was coming, and Allison backed away from sight as beaming headlights streamed into our still, dark apartment. I hugged her long and tight in the corner where the door hinged so as not to be seen. I left in tears on what was supposed to be a magical trip. Oddly enough, circumstance aside, it was one of the best trips we had ever taken as a family. Only, the "circumstances" part (my identity, my truth, and my Allison) was a pretty big thing to put aside.

I was nervous when I got into the car, but rather quickly, I could tell that everyone was making efforts to be on their best, non-argumentative behavior. My sister was unfailingly supportive, my dad always quick to diffuse arguments, and I think my mom was just wanting to return to normalcy on neutral ground. All these things combined to make the best four days I'd had with them in a year. There were some common trigger topics that we had to avoid: politics, religion, and anything that might in any way lead to a gay-themed issue. We were planning on going to a Broadway show, so I was hoping someone bought an extra ticket for the elephant.

My dad graciously booked two separate rooms in our Times Square hotel, so my sister and I would have separate space to get ready in the mornings, and plenty of time to decompress at the end of the day. Dad spoiled us. Although my dad would never be superficial enough to think he could buy togetherness, I know the trip was an effort to piece our family back together after a tumultuous year.

On Christmas Eve night, as we walked down 5th Avenue *ooooing* and *ahhhhing* at all the ornate shop windows, my mom mentioned wanting to go to a midnight mass service. My ears perked up because I knew she had been on a church hiatus for quite some time. Jumping at the chance to enjoy church once again with my mom, I immediately began looking up mass services nearby. Barely three blocks away, a church called St. Thomas was opening its doors for Christmas Eve service. I began leading the way down the crowded street, excited at the thought of sharing a worship service with my family. When we got closer, we noticed that the church was undergoing some renovations and thus surrounded by scaffolding.

"Wait, what church is this?" my mom asked as she peered through the construction.

I reiterated, "St. Thomas!"

"I know that, but what denomination?" she inquired.

Then I realized where the conversation was headed.

"It's an Episcopal church," I said reluctantly.

"I would rather go to a Catholic mass." Her voice was surprisingly civil and non-confrontational.

"Why?" I (shouldn't have) asked.

"I'm just not in agreement with the Episcopal church like I thought I was." She was matter-of-fact, and her efforts at curbing the bitterness were pretty commendable. After her initial malice toward the church, this was a vast improvement. I was proud of the grace she showed in that moment and decided not to press the issue. In the end, we were too tired to stay up for mass anyhow.

■ ■ ■

Christmas morning was so different, but it was a refreshing change. Instead of running to a tree full of color-coordinated packages, we woke up and met in the hotel restaurant for brunch. It felt like a very adult thing to do. What's more, Dad ordered us all a mimosa to celebrate the day—which was a big deal because he never liked drinking alcohol in front of his kids. So we toasted the $16 mimosas, ate from an astronomically priced buffet, and laughed until we cried. The waiter took a photo as we toasted the last sips of our bubbly juice. I still look back at that photo and wish that I could recapture that happiness within my family again.

Later that day, after some bus tours around the boroughs, we were dropped back off in Times Square. We all went our separate ways to do some shopping before getting ready to go to the Broadway play that evening. Rebekah dove headfirst into three-story clothing shops while Mom and Dad perused a watch store nearby. I shoved my cold hands into my pockets, tucked my hair back into my toboggan, and took a long walk to the toy store, thinking about the turtle dove ornament Kevin shared with the pigeon lady in the park.

As I walked, I looked around at what was probably the quietest day in New York City. The view was cast with a sharp, cold gray color, but flashing marquis still shone as if it were already New Year's Eve. Funny how only seven days separated such serenity from a time when one million people would be stacked on top of one another to watch a ball drop. I'd honestly never had the desire to be in Times Square on New Year's Eve. Not to sound geriatric, but the thought of standing in the same spot for eight hours and having to create a tactical potty plan never sounded worth those sixty seconds of hysteria. The confetti always looked fun, though. Like sprinkles on a cupcakes—rather unnecessary, but they sure do add to the experience.

Seconds after these thoughts passed my mind, I looked up to see a tent filled with people. Everyone was gathered at a small table, writing. Behind them I could see a wall of confetti labeled "Hopes and Dreams" in large, vintage font.

"Ma'am," called one of the staff members in the tent, "would you like to write a message on a piece of confetti that will drop in Times Square next week? It's a free project!"

I was skeptical of anything "free." Nevertheless, I walked under the tent to escape the wind. Turns out, it *was* free. I dug through the pile of fragile, paper sprinkles and pulled out my favorite color, green. I stood there contemplating my wish with an earnestness that made me seem like I actually expected it to come true. *Should I write one profound word, a phrase, a tiny essay?* People came and went while I continued to stand there. I'm sure the staff was thinking, *Lady! Just write "win the lottery" or something*, but I take these type of things very seriously.

Then I proceeded to write out my heart's desire— my desire to have my relationship with Allison flourish and for my mother to accept it one day.

# 29

## EQUAL LOVE AND MARGARITAS

The holidays came and went, but things didn't really change. The magical span of those few days gave me hope that our family could reassemble from the ashes, but it was still too soon. Life was moving on regardless of what I wanted, so I tried to keep up and not to let my feet sink into the murky dregs of depression. My little sister had made the healthy decision to leave our hometown. She had been caught in the middle, and I ached for her happiness.

I met Rebekah in a new city with her new friends and a new lease on life (and on an apartment). She was going to go back to college, start work, and chase after complete independence she'd yet to experience back home. I was beaming with pride as I helped her unload the moving truck. After a thunderstorm, what seemed like a thousand boxes, and moving two couches up two flights of stairs, we were all famished. I suggested margaritas to celebrate, so we all hopped in the car and wheeled into a place that advertised, "In queso emergency, stop here!"

Some salsa and margaritas later, the subject of my coming out came up in conversation. I can't remember how.

"So there's something I never told you," Rebekah said.

The table got quiet.

"What? What is it?" I asked.

"The night you called me and came out to me, I was so overwhelmed and happy. The second I got off the phone, I went to a tattoo parlor." She smiled that little girl smile and shrugged her shoulders. "I got the equality symbol. It was for you."

"Why didn't you ever tell me that?"

"Well, life got crazy. It was my silent tribute to you, and I guess I just never got around to telling you about it."

My eyes welled up. "Well I want to see it! Let me see!"

"It's on my ribs, kinda under my bra strap," she explained. "I'd have to lift up my shirt, and I don't…"

"No, no, no, I want to see it! No one's looking!"

After some coaxing, she lifted up the side of her shirt. There, in simple black ink, was a small heart with the equality symbol nestled inside it.

"It's so beautiful," I said and buried my head in my hands. I could've blamed it on the alcohol, but I was crying because it was one of the sweetest things anyone had ever done for me.

■ ■ ■

When we were kids, my sister and I were quite the team. Being seven years apart, we fell naturally into caretaker/ protégé roles rather than becoming rivals. I pushed her toward structure and maturity while she kept me honest and young. Since we homeschooled, we were more than siblings. We were classmates, playmates, fellow explorers, and adventurers. It wasn't uncommon for our neighbors to look out their windows and see little Rebekah flying down a grassy hill in her wagon, sporting all manner of padding and the fear of God on her face. I, the operator of the scheme, stood gazing from the top of the hill, pleased that I was making my little sister "tough."

Rebekah was a willing participant in all my escapades growing up. Wagon roller coasters were just the start. We would Oregon Trail around the yard, scavenging for leaves and pinecones that would serve as sustenance. I spent hours printing animal fact sheets and coloring pages for our "Endangered Species Club," which one member begrudgingly attended. She would sit and listen to my speeches full of conservation jargon, color some obligatory lines on a bandicoot, then scamper back to her dolls. She waited patiently as I changed my American Girl doll back into her horse-riding knickers because I liked pants better than the dresses (shocker). She watched as I paired all our Beanie Babies into partners, making sure the couples were diversified. The seal and walrus didn't *necessarily* have to be together, nor did all the cats need to be together. It seemed perfectly okay that the leopard and seal were mates (again, shocker).

Childhood was euphoric for us. We didn't go to school, so we weren't often made to feel that the conventional way was the essential way. We had our own style, our own flare, and there are photos and home videos to prove it. We memorized scripture and stood on the hearth to quote it in unison to an audience of two: our parents. We made silly home videos pretending to be newscasters, chefs, and infomercial salespeople. I can't remember a time when my sister wasn't supportive of my hare-brained ideas and just plain supportive of *me*. So why was I paralyzed with fear to tell her I was gay? I suddenly wasn't the "tough" one anymore. We'd had dozens of conversations that danced around the subject like a game of Taboo, but I'd never actually admitted my feelings. I can't begin to express my relief when I heard her affirmation on the phone that day.

"Well I already knew, Meredith," she said, as if I had just reminded her that my eyes were blue.

"Really?" I was almost speechless.

"God, yes."

"How?"

"Let's see," she said, pausing to feign thought, "remember that Halloween all the cousins dressed up like princesses and you were looming in the background dressed as Jason from *Friday the 13th*? Yeah, dead give away. Pardon the pun."

I laughed hysterically amidst happy tears.

She continued, "You cried when mom made you go bra shopping. I honestly think you cursed puberty. Let's see, you played street hockey by yourself in the driveway and did your own play-by-play announcing. You never carried a purse, and when you did, the only thing you put in it was chapstick and pocket knives. You've never had a boyfriend. You collected NBA trading cards and didn't put any curl-taming product in your hair until you were nineteen, and that was only because we all *highly* suggested it."

I was still laughing.

"Meredith, for real. You are *so* gay."

My heart was at ease.

# 30

## BRAVE ENOUGH

The new year dawned, and it was Allison's birthday week-end. After an evening with her family and too much cake, we left for the hour-long journey home. As we merged onto the interstate, I received a text from a girl named Alex, whom I had met through a mutual friend on social media. We texted casually and had only met in person once, but for some reason, we had confronted very personal hurdles in the few conversations we'd shared. Two months before I met Allison, Alex had poured her heart out about her own, very similar questions regarding sexuality. Like me, she had tried dating guys but was always skeptical of them past a second date. We both connected emotionally with girls, and let's face it, were just much more attracted to them. We were also both raised with very strict and traditional values, and though this helped shape our character, it also smoth-ered things the heart would express. Alex told me about a girl she had been seeing on and off again. The off-again portion only happened when both girls hit a rocky valley where they questioned their eternity. Inevitably they would reconnect, thinking it a "fall back into temptation." The truth was, they loved each other. The fact that they had to smother and *deny* that love was the cause of their infidelity and needless searching. I had found myself without words when Alex told me this. It would have been a perfect time to come out to *someone*, lest I be eaten up with confusion and loneliness. But I'd held my tongue, too terrified to even hear myself utter words I had suppressed for so long. Instead, I just gave her a cookie-cutter answer: *I understand. That's gotta be tough.*

Imagine my surprise when I heard from her this night, a year later. In fact, imagine her surprise when she heard I was in a relationship with a girl after I'd eluded to no such thing in our earlier conversations. I'd always felt a bit guilty for allowing my apprehension to hold the truth captive. Perhaps it would have helped Alex to know that there was another soul in our conservative, red state who was grappling to hold onto the title of "gay Christian." That first opportunity had passed, but here I suddenly had another. Alex and a group of her friends, among them the girl she was crazy about, were at a local sports bar. She asked if we wanted to meet up. Allison and I had had a long, socially exhausting weekend, so detouring from the road to our own cozy bed was enough to make me think twice. Then I thought about how badly I had craved mentors. It was imperative that I go.

We drove to the bar, on the other side of the city, and walked into the loud and glaring section closest to the bar. The place was not exactly an introvert's ideal scene, and I wondered if the atmosphere would even be conducive to a conversation. I was under the impression that Alex would have questions regarding mine and Allison's relationship, and how we had managed to be publicly partnered (and happy) in a small town. Then again, I considered that she might also just want to hang out, seeing from a distance how a supposedly taboo relationship could indeed work, be healthy, *and* be God-honoring.

I knew when Alex introduced Allison to everyone as my girlfriend and then emphatically as "the youth minister at their *church*" that she wanted to show that being gay and being Christian were terms that could coexist. The conversation was suddenly a safe space whirling with questions, revelations, and hopeful smiles. I told them that my coming out was nothing short of a disaster, and I told them that there was most likely no way to rock the stubborn and traditional opinions of some Bible Belt Christians. Although I appreciated *some* of the things the southern Baptist Christian tradition had taught me (mainly my familiarity with scripture), I felt as if I was merely reading a Bible stories from children's book—the kind with colorful illustrations and interactive pages full of zippers and crinkly paper. Moving to the Episcopal church (where intellect was invited) felt like shifting from a coloring book to a scholarly paper annotated by Biblical players and intellects of their day. I explained that some people found it impossible to slough off the more fictional, irrelevant parts of their religion and look at it through a more academic lens. Without that willingness, there could not be a breakthrough past the age-old "agree to disagree" pact. At that point, there must be a humble release of control, else we would all drive ourselves nuts.

"Staying in the Bible Belt is difficult," I admitted candidly. "But don't give up. Not on yourself, and not on the people who might reject you."

As I listened to myself speaking to these girls, I heard a conviction in my voice that I didn't even recognize. I was suddenly more proud and assured than I had ever been.

"You've struggled with that theology for a long time," Allison said to me after we left the bar that night, "but for the first time, I heard *belief* in your voice."

She was right. I finally felt brave enough.

# 31

## DON'T SHOOT THE MUSE

Halfway through writing this story, my confidence felt so fatigued that I contemplated stopping altogether. I would go through ebbs and flows of guilt and pain as I began to write about my coming out and the many hurtful things said along the way. I was filled with words, flowing with passionate ways to makes sense of the mess in my head, but instead of writing candidly and pressing my raw feelings onto paper, I wrote as if someone were looking over my shoulder. I wrote as if a dark and cloudy disclaimer loomed over my work, protecting my family's reputation and shielding their confusion.

I grew up riding the waves of family anxieties, being that ever-present source of level-headed comfort for everyone else. I practiced obedience as if it was a sport or piano lessons. Even as a college student, I dutifully called home when I left and arrived at places. I asked for permission to stay after class and hang out with a friend. I was granted an 11 p.m. curfew on occasion to see a band play on my college campus. On my 21st birthday, I was in a Victorian poetry class until 7pm then met my family at Cracker Barrel. Alcohol was a non-negotiable, and I adhered to that. Let's be honest, I loved Cracker Barrel biscuits, too. I always thought I was quirky, odd, and unconventional in my thinking about all these things. I wasn't, though. I was just gay and closeted, and this shattered the perfection of societal norms that engulfed me.

Why did I consider writing these things only in a journal and stopping the book process entirely? Because of my Marmee, the dear person who read *Little Women* aloud to me. She was the person who relished that I related to Josephine March, the book's resident tomboy, writer, and dreamer. Through my mother's tireless voice, I learned not to let the sun go down on my anger (even if my sister burned my beloved manuscript), and I learned not to let convention tell me how to live my life. Unfortunately, my mother let many suns set on her anger, but I can't let that quell my voice. Even if it takes a thousand sunrises, I will wait for the one that brings reconciliation.

At a pivotal time during my writing, I picked up the book *Big Magic*, written by my hero, Elizabeth Gilbert. I had met her a few years ago at a book-signing in Maine, and she was everything I had ever dreamed she would be—elegant and poised, authentic and humble. Her words, both spoken and written, were so wonderfully woven together that, even after hearing them for the first time, they blanketed me with a comfort akin to a nursery rhyme or poem I'd heard a hundred times. Even if she doesn't ever know it, I feel that we are kindred spirits—the kind that Anne of Green Gables talked about: true, bosom friends. In *Big Magic*, Liz attributes all human creativity to an active, intangible muse who partners with human hosts. Ideas run rampant, searching for a receptive mind but, if neglected, will float away in search of another readied spirit.

The idea for writing this book, and beyond that, my intentions for the reader, hit me like a glass of cold water in the face. As the idea woke me, it then washed warm over me, latching itself to my very soul. Thus, as Liz says, I signed a contract with my idea, and I flung myself into my writing. I let the idea and outline take shape without much of my own direction, but as my idea began to require more and more honesty from me, I slowly and timidly took back the reins, shunning my poor muse in the process. I would erase pages and pages worth of honesty that had been so painstakingly given to me. I masked the painful truth with wordiness. There sat my muse in a dusty corner of my mind, watching me struggle through passages about my family. The muse had already eloquently painted an honest depiction of my experiences, albeit painfully tender, but I decided to dilute them all. My muse, considering this to be disrespectful to our agreement, let me squander my time away on hours of useless work. For a few months, I hardly wrote at all. Just as my idea was about to pack its bags and vacate my mind forever, I called it back and asked for one more chance.

I re-read the letters, messages, and emails. Recalling the pain was one of the hardest things I've ever had to do. Maybe one day we could relinquish the theological differences, too, and embrace each other despite them. Deep down, I still hoped. But until that time, why should I conceal how all those words affected me? The words *shaped* me. It was difficult, but I finally surrendered my stoic, passive approach to writing about what happened to me. There are those few-and-far-between stories of complete acceptance in the Bible Belt, but those stories weren't mine, and I couldn't wait around to *become* that story. With every word I penned, I prayed that my authenticity would bring my family back.

The moment I pressed onward and thought, *what the hell*, was the moment I began to write freely again. My idea began to swirl and frolic again, forgiving me for almost denying it the chance of being its spokesperson.

# 32

## SILENT TOO LONG

As newfound confidence in befriending my muse continued to grow, I kept feeling more and more compelled to
speak out on issues that affected me and others. Little did I
know, a huge opportunity to reject silence awaited me one
random, rainy morning.

It was close to mine and Allison's two year anniver-
sary. I woke up to a text from my friend Zac—just a link
with no text attached. This wasn't altogether uncommon.
Zac often kept me updated on fun political happenings
by sending me the least convoluted articles on any given
subject. I always liked the condensed version of stories, especially ones involving the fiasco that was the 2016 presi-
dential election. I clicked on the link and waited for the
article to load. I saw that I was being to directed to a local,
Alabama news source. When the headline popped up, I
couldn't believe my eyes. The title read, *Bisexual daughter of*
*Rick & Bubba host will no longer stay silent.*

I scanned the article with my mouth hanging open, a rush of emotions overwhelming me. Before even finishing the article, I did a Google search for Brandi. I happened upon her acting website, glad to see her seemingly happy and successful in the northeast, away from the less-affirming south. Clicking on the contact box, I was skeptical that I would reach her. Sometimes I felt like website inquiries floated alone in cyberspace. Either way, I poured out my soul in that contact box, using each character to the fullest. I applauded her bravery, gave her a brief synopsis of my story, and left her with what I hoped to be a sense of camaraderie with this person in her home state—someone fighting for her.

The next couple of days were remarkable (with some good ol' fashioned bedlam and mayhem mixed in). Brandi responded to my message, receiving my words with a heart wide open. During these same few days, Rick rallied his prejudices and, with Bible in hand, went live on his news stream to crusade against this new opposition, his own daughter. In this hour-long segment, I watched as Rick twisted insubstantial and outdated Biblical evidence to reject and disown his child. My heart experienced a righteous fury unlike any I'd ever felt. Using the rush, I incited my normal coping mechanism, writing. I addressed Rick head-on in an open letter blog, weighing whether or not I should discredit my spiritual, longsuffering-type approach with the use of profanity. For the sake of the blog, I reigned it in. But for my book, I'd like to say—don't fuck with a writer.

The following is the blog in full text:

*Rick,*

*Nearly two years ago, you replied to an email from my mother. She was mourning the loss of her daughter— that's me— because I am gay. She came to you, a radio talkshow host, to ask about the security of my salvation. You wondered why I would "redefine intimacy with no conviction" because "the Bible is clear." You talked about me as if I had a wretched illness, telling my mother to "pray, pray, pray that I love Christ more than my sexuality." The reason I know these things is because she forwarded your conversation to me. It was actually among the last of communication attempts between us. Never have I felt so vulnerable, wrongly berated, unable to defend myself, and frankly, so sad I ached. But I still had hope that she would hear and be gracious enough to understand my side one day.*

*Imagine my utter shock and excitement when I woke up to see Brandi's article on Friday. I immediately found a way to message your daughter, to reach out for some sort of empathy and applaud her outright bravery. Coming out in a southern, Christian family is grueling. But it's exceedingly difficult trying to cling to that same precious faith as it is being simultaneously ripped from our hands. During the most tumultuous time of my life, when I* needed my God the most, you made me feel outcast and vile. I had just begun to heal. Seeing Brandi's news and corresponding with her was even more soothing to my soul. But then you targeted us on your show. My mother was listening— listening to your broad admonitions and expansive vocabulary about redemption— and because of that, you've probably sabotaged my chances of making things okay.

We are on the same side, Rick. I am a professing Christian wishing to be in equal communion with my brothers and sisters, yet you've shunned me. I'm not a prodigal. Please don't assign me to that role. I didn't want to leave. But no one will listen long enough to hear me. There may be division in your household (like you & Matthew 10 mentions,) but don't assume yourself equipped enough to testify that Brandi, me or any gay person has caused the division— lest this be projecting your own bias and interpretation upon scripture— which we silly, hippie Jesus millennials aren't supposed to do, correct? What if, just perhaps, those of us gay Christians (who haven't been rejected and scorned beyond repair) are being called to reveal what the Bible truly says? Not reinterpret, reinvent, or gloss-over, but truly speak the message of Christ's inclusive love.

Here's the part where you say, "but the Bible is clear and consistent on homosexuality." While on the air, you said you wouldn't justify Brandi all the way to hell, but did you explain the verses you think are responsible for such a bold statement? You said Brandi couldn't even back up her stance. Well here I am, and I'm ready to back her up. If you want me to break it down verse by verse, let's get together for coffee later. For now, we need to know the difference between re-inventing and expounding. C.S. Lewis himself equates Theology (the science of God) to exploration and practicality rather than just emotion. "If you do not listen to Theology," he said, "that will not mean that you have no ideas about God. It will mean that you have a lot of wrong ones — bad, muddled, out-of-date ideas." C.S Lewis described some of our fundamental dependencies on stories, or "novelties," in the Bible as being rooted in ignorance— akin to the type of retrogression that allowed people to think the earth flat. You see, theology expounds on what is already written, citing contextually that all references to homosexual behavior are texts exposing the sins of lust, idolatry, rape, and prostitution— **not** condemning a God-centered, committed, same-sex relationship. Nothing has been changed. It's all there.

In fact, in Romans chapter 1, Paul describes a sinful nature that continues to corrupt and produce even more sin. In my short time of being out and meeting other gay Christians, I have yet to meet a more intrinsically kind, holy, Christ-led group *of people with such zeal for the Spirit. Morgan Guyton, in his blog Mercy Not Sacrifice poses similar arguments: "So when you encounter gay Christians who are plainly not 'filled with every kind of wickedness, evil, covetousness, malice... envy, murder, strife, deceit, craftiness... [and who aren't] gossips, slanderers, God-haters, insolent, haughty, boastful, inventors of evil, etc (v. 29-31), it seems very legitimate to ask whether the 'shameless acts' Paul is talking about in verses 27-28 were sinful for a reason other than the genders involved (like promiscuity, adultery, recklessness, etc.)"*

*The real issue here is fear. The opposite of love is not hate— it is fear. I know you don't hate Brandi, you don't even hate her choices. Perhaps there really is something to the term, "homophobia." You are frightened of them because you've not searched deep enough to understand. You've not searched enough in scripture, in your own heart, or within communities unlike your own. You couldn't even muster within yourself to say the word **gay**. Instead, you stumbled around the subject with shame, talking about her "decision" and "her own journey."*

*So, like the prodigal story, there will be people topping a hill to come back home, but it won't be because of a squandered inheritance or a rebellious heart. We as professing Christians, no matter who we are, have already inherited the kingdom of God. We are just waiting for our families to celebrate*

*with us. As we crawl out from under the burden of
a foregone construct into the new light of Christ, we
are "no longer male and female… we are all one in
Christ Jesus" (Galatians 3:28)*

*Peace,*
*Meredith*

It all started to make sense—Rick's outspoken, on-air homophobia, his cut-rate sermon email to my mother, and
now the deluge of shame as he scrambled to protect his
precious platform. He was projecting an intense and bitter
fear he had harbored deep within himself. It suddenly became real to him, and Rick was at a crossroad. Brandi had
outed (no pun intended) her father's selfish reaction, and
Rick, being so afraid that Brandi's honesty would compromise his radio show, made a calculated move to satisfy
raving, fundamentalist fans rather than take a moment to
listen to his daughter.

In less than 48 hours, my blog had been shared innumerable times and the view count neared 12,000. My
inbox was inundated by comments ranging from people
slinging Sodom & Gomorrah verses to soothing consola-
tions from complete strangers. To make my blog accessible
to the public, that meant opening myself up to ridicule—
even from my mom. At that time, my blog was the only
method with which my mom could still contact with me,
and I knew from the comments that she had yet to begin
healing. And I wondered if she ever would.

# 33

## LONG FUSE

Allowing myself to dwell on the derisive words that have been said to me over the years regarding my sexuality has left me on the brink of self-loathing. *How have I driven people to feel such pain, to wield words so mercilessly?* I ask myself on numerous occasions. Hypnotized by the rebuke, I began to believe the words then grow increasingly angrier because of them. I don't like the feeling of anger. I don't feel it very often, but the coming out process has caused me to experience it much more than I ever have. Settling anger and defusing any confrontation was always my strong suit, a trait I was silently proud of, but it turns out that quelling hurt is, in fact, super unhealthy. In a therapy session not too long ago, a priest asked me about anger. I immediately dismissed it, gloating that I handled anger better than anyone because I don't reveal it. Revealing anger is wrong. I saw the effects of that as a child. Outward anger hurt people. Outward anger still haunted me.

"Don't you see," implored the priest, "that suppressing something as powerful as anger might cause you to become the exact embodiment of a trait you despise? A character lashing out irrationally? One day enough will be enough. You have an extremely long fuse, Meredith, but once it's lit. . ." His voice trailed off, and we shared a good laugh.

He was right. Hurt was collecting inside me like a dormant volcano, cornered in the most vulnerable parts of my heart like a skittish dog, and flickering slowly along that seemingly endless fuse. I never thought I would receive advice about anger. It nearly hurt my pride to address it. *Me? Me dealing with anger? My job is to deflect and absorb anger, not feel it.* According to the rules, though, I am actually *allowed* to feel it, to embrace, to name it, to direct it.

"Use some methods to defuse it. Be expressive, write in a journal, talk about it with a therapist," the priest said.

In other words, I needed always to be one step ahead of frustration. And boy have I taken that advice on writing. *Commence writing manifesto.*

So now, heartened by this new, let's call it, "license to rage," I am expressing how I feel. And I will do it until the day I die— with a mixture of as much grace and intensity as possible. Like the poet Dylan Thomas said in his poem "Do not go gentle into that good night":

> *Old age should burn and rave at close of day;*
> *Rage, rage against the dying of the light.*

In fact, the words of this life-affirming poem were pinned to my back as I walked with a million women down the streets of Washington D.C. Purpose, pride, and my head held high were symptoms of a newfound expression—an expression which allowed me to cope with anger in a worthy way. Participating in the Women's March on Washington and doing other "liberal snowflake" things weren't an act of defiance or a rebellion against all I was taught. They were symbols that I was no longer afraid to have an opinion and be different.

When I was no longer afraid what people thought, I cut my hair. It was the most liberating feeling on earth. Of course you would've thought I had amputated an essential body part. Not only does hair grow back, but it also doesn't carry the emblem that some people traditionally place upon it— specifically long hair. While I'm only cutting my hair to try a fun, new style, those in opposition *mourn* my hair. Long hair secured my place in a staunch gender role, sending a beacon to all eligible bachelors. Naturally, once I cut my hair, I was hopelessly and irrevocably gay. I even got my laminated Certificate of Lesbian Authenticity in the mail that very week. But for *real* folks. I already wore my hair up 90% of the time, effectively hiding the quality of my mane anyhow. With it short, I am now actually enjoying my wildish curls and, let's be honest, a pretty cool fade, too.

Humor has definitely helped me along the way. Its another outlet for my frustrations, really. Luckily, I'm surrounded with a group of friends who publicly point out the hypocrisies and help turn my sad tears into the laughter ones. Like this one from my friend Zac in response to a rather angsty and misinformed blog commenter: "How about Deuteronomy 22:11, huh? *Thou shalt not wear a garment of diverse sorts, as of woolen and linen together.* Guess my cotton blend sweater is gonna burn in hell with me."

*Guess my cotton blend sweater is gonna burn in hell with me.* I bust out laughing every time I think about it. Then I'm simultaneously reassured that I'm not the only one who can find silly contradictions in the Bible but still value the gospel— and myself. Anytime I see hurtful words or think hurtful thoughts, I just make an effort to change them, rewrite them, *reclaim them.*

> *I am reconstructing my dreams for the future.*
> *I am finally finding where I fit in.*
> *I am guarding my soul.*

# 34

## SPIRIT ANIMALS

When I was a little kid, I was a professional card-giver. If there was an occasion, I was making someone a card. Most of the recipients were from church, because that's where I spent most of my time. Being a rather perceptive child, I quietly watched the adults, listening to their conversations and reading their emotions. I didn't much like interacting with kids my own age, so being a quiet bystander to adult conversations was my favorite. During Wednesday night dinner at church, I would sit in my mom's shadow while kids frolicked around playing tag. I listened to people's stories about their families, tragedies, and joys. I was often so overcome with respect and sympathy that I'd spend the church service sketching or composing notes on the offering envelopes. My mom was gracious to let me waste church literature like that, but to me, I guess it wasn't a waste. I loved writing letters, drawing pictures, or even just copying encouraging scripture on a scratch piece of paper to brighten someone's day. When I got older and learned how to build and bind books, I would create stories for people I loved—dedicate it to them even.

One time, during one of those church night conversations, I heard that our pianist's husband had been diagnosed with cancer. I was suddenly burdened with so much grief for them both, especially the pianist whom I adored like a grandmother. I would often watch her play after services until the sanctuary was empty, then dart away before she could see me. When I heard about her husband's illness, I immediately began planning the care package I wanted to give them. Of course, the only thing to do was to draw them some forest animals with my best colored pencils. I worked all week on a drawing of some woodland creatures and an accompanying card. I had been taking art lessons and was learning how to blend colors and improve my shading; I'd even learned a trick to keep the pencil from smearing (a light coat of hairspray). I was elated the next week at Wednesday night dinner when I approached them with my drawing. I remember being nervous and not knowing what to say besides, "I'm sorry you're sick. I am praying for you." I scurried off, beaming from heart to soul thinking that I must have made them the happiest people in the world.

As I grew up, I also grew discouraged in my projects. So many letters, care packages, and careful drawings were received with a patronizing "thank you" or nothing at all. I was, after all, just a child drawing pictures and then running off to hide behind her mom. But was it that simple?

Even I didn't understand at the time. Not to say that I was only seeking accolades or acknowledgment, but I was craving affirmation. I was using my medium, my love language, and calling out for affection. I wanted to *matter*.

Too often I reprimanded myself for wanting to matter, though. I was supposed to be satisfied with God's love, not preoccupied by worldly desires or acceptance. I grew up thinking it selfish, this desire to be loved. So in a repressed effort to seek it, I continued pouring myself into friends, mentors, family members, even strangers, projecting what I desired most: to be someone's priority. I wanted to be loved, and I didn't know how to ask for it. As life progressed, not only was I afraid to ask for love, I was confused as in which form I wanted to *have* love.

Imagine the completeness of my joy when I met Allison, the first person to ever allow me to see love in all its facets: reciprocated, prized, and indispensable. Loving her was finally finding an insatiable vessel to hold the love I had to give. My heart, in turn, is saturated every day with similar joys. I keep her notes or cards scattered around to remind me that I matter, and that it's okay to want to feel that way.

"Will you tell me a story?" Allison asked one night as I was falling asleep. I had noticed she'd been tossing and turning a lot. "I drank coffee way too late today."

"Sure, what kind of story?"

"Anything!" she said and snuggled closer to me.

"I don't know any stories by heart, really." I paused for a minute, almost nervous because impromptu storytelling wasn't really my specialty. I was more of a pen and paper kind of gal.

"You can make something up," she reassured me. "I just want to hear your voice and calm my mind so I can shake these zoomies." (Zoomies was a word we used to describe our dog Keeper's sporadic and silly scampering around the house.)

"Alright, let's see."

Only weeks into our relationship, Allison had happened upon a caterpillar on the sidewalk. It was the iconic, storybook caterpillar—bright green with curious, prickly hairs searching around, flecks of orange accessorizing its squishy body. I categorized everything as "bug," shuddering at any creepy crawler, while Allison jumped at any chance to examine them up close and personal-like. On this day, she did just that. Dropping to the ground and crouching nearly eye level to the vibrant creature, she said, "Caterpillars are my spirit animal."

"Why?" I asked, assuming it was related to a metamorphosis theme.

"Well, it's not what you'd think. It has nothing to do with the butterfly thing, actually."

"Huh," I replied and reflected for a moment. I tried to think of what else could *possibly* be appealing about a caterpillar.

"I like them because they're never in a hurry. They are patient, present, creative…" her voice trailed off as it often did when she was distracted by something beautiful.

"I think my spirit animal is a fox," I said. I had always liked the mysterious allure of the fox. But like Allison, I didn't necessarily want to embrace the customary stereotype of the fox as sneaky and cunning. The fox was quiet yet vibrant, and it seemed to have an innate guidance which made it agile, wise, and quite mesmerizing to me.

I vividly remember the day Allison found that caterpillar. Her ideas about its symbolism resonated so deeply with her, and it was something she was so passionately sure about— unconventionally so. From that day on, we talked about our spirit animals, pointed them out (stuffed animals, graphic images, real-life, and otherwise), and used their emojis in text messages. So the night Allison asked me to tell her a story, I knew it would feature the fox and the caterpillar.

> *Once upon a time, in a cool and shaded wood, there lived a shy fox. Even so, the little fox had an adventurous spirit. She would peek from her den to make sure there were no other woodland creatures around before emerging to play. Then, when all was clear and quiet, the fox would frolic, jump, and race among the trees.*
>
> *One particularly venturesome day, the fox frolicked all the way to the edge of the wood.*
>
> *"Perhaps I could take one step out of my home and find a new friend," she said, lifting her paw. Following the whim, she pounced into a new adventure.*

Little fox travelled the world, never once looking back. She met all kinds of new creatures. Tall ones, bright ones, formidable ones, smelly ones, and fast ones. They were, for the most part, very charming creatures, but somehow the fox knew that they wouldn't be around forever—they were just there for that particular adventure.

The little fox grew weary of her adventure and wanted to be back in the cool, shaded wood where everything and everyone was familiar. When she got back, everything was the same as she had left it. The trees were a little taller and her den seemed a little smaller, but it was nice to be home. Fox settled back into her shy ways, hiding from forest creatures and frolicking about in the twilight hours.

One day, as the little fox scampered back to her den, she felt a sudden feeling. It was a hollow, cloudy feeling in her heart. Had she lost something? Maybe that was it. So the little fox walked slowly along, her paw-steps silent on the cool, damp earth. Her keen eyes scanned the ground, looking for something. For what, she did not know.

Then she saw it. There, on a fern sat a contented caterpillar. The vibrant, bright-eyed creature was inching around and didn't see the little fox's shadow.

"Hello, Caterpillar," said the customarily shy fox. "I was looking for you!"

"Excuse me?" replied the perplexed insect. "I'm afraid we haven't met. I'm new here in the wood."

"Oh I know," the fox said. "I was just walking home and suddenly felt as if I had lost something. Then I found you!"

"Well perhaps we should be friends," suggested the caterpillar. "I'd quite like that."

And so the pair were thereafter inseparable.

Caterpillar, as pocket-sized as she was, had a big heart. Fox sometimes thought she'd take flight with the liveliness she possessed. She didn't let the large world intimidate her. Instead, she took life one step at a time, soaking in all the wonderfulness of it.

"You know, Fox," said caterpillar, "I feel like we're all bursting with something colorful. Maybe it's creativity, maybe it's kindness, or maybe it's just wanting to be a loving presence for another creature. Whatever the case, there's no need to be in a hurry."

"We should probably share that colorfulness," the Fox said, surprised to be suggesting something outside her comfort-den. "But I'm so shy."

"Remarkable idea, Fox! Don't worry, just stick with me."

Caterpillar taught Fox how to meet new people and find common ground. There were grasshoppers and rabbits, but both hopped. There were birds and butterflies, but they both could fly.

Fox learned so much from Caterpillar.

Fox, though shy, relentlessly chased after adventure and an elusive muse. It was hard to have such expressive feelings with such a timid spirit, but she somehow expressed herself with words and a silent drive to move—her body, mind, and spirit.

"You know, Caterpillar," said the fox. "Sometimes the colorfulness in our mind gets all tangled. We have to find a way to convey our beautiful souls and set our ideas free!"

"We should probably go exploring," suggested Caterpillar. "But I'm not good at frolicking about the wood."

"Marvelous idea, Caterpillar! Don't worry, just stick with me."

Fox lowered her head and let Caterpillar inch onto her slender, red nose.

Together they scampered, jumped, ran, soared, flipped, and frolicked all over the wood until the sun began its nightly retreat behind the mountain peaks. Fox ambled her way through some trails, crossed a suspended bridge, traversed a creek bed and the mouth of a waterfall, and finally reached an edge.

"Where are we?" asked Caterpillar as they neared a precipice.

"*A colorful place,*" Fox answered. "*The setting sun, pines glistening with dew, glass-like flecks bouncing from the riverbed... They calm my mind and help me understand my own thoughts.*"

*Together they sat and watched the sunset.*

"*I found it,*" whispered Fox.

"*What did you find?*" asked Caterpillar, keeping her eyes on the sunset. "*Your muse? Untangled thoughts? Bravery?*"

"*No,*" sighed Fox. "*I found you.*" Fullness and warmth suddenly filled Fox. It burned red as her coat.

"*Can we watch all the sunsets together, my Fox?*" asked the caterpillar softly.

"*I'd like that.*"

*And so they did.*

I remember falling a little deeper in love with Allison as she made that cute "falling asleep" noise with her mouth and her head fell heavy on my chest. To her, I mattered. And despite what happened next, we were together. And maybe that's *all* that mattered.

# 35

## LIGHT PERPETUAL

I was getting ready for work when I got a call from my dad.

"What are you doing?" he asked abruptly.

"Nothing," I answered. "What's wrong?" I asked because I knew something was.

"Your mom just called and said they rushed Papaw to the hospital. It doesn't sound good, so I want you to just prepare yourself, okay?"

"Alright."

He continued talking, but my brain filtered the details and for a while I heard only muffled sound. Before he hung up, he said, "I'm on my way there now. I will text you when I find out something."

Ten days prior, my Papaw had gone outside on a rainy evening to check the mail. He was on his way to pick up a pizza for dinner. When he opened the mailbox, a bird flew out. It startled him so badly that he fell backward into the street. With a broken hip, Papaw sat alone in the rain. A neighbor finally noticed and ran out to help. Life wasn't the same after that. The whole scenario— the pizza, the bird, the rain— overtakes me with grief each time I hear it. The sweet simplicity of going to get a pizza, being frightened by something so fluke as a bird, and then sitting alone and struggling in the rain. The vision of this is etched in my brain in a place where only grief lurks.

We found out that Papaw needed immediate surgery to repair the hip, but his preexisting health problems made it difficult for doctors to stabilize him for such a traumatic procedure. After a couple days of sitting and waiting in pain, he was admitted to surgery and against unfortunate odds, came through wonderfully. After a few days at the hospital, Papaw was moved to a nursing home to begin rehab. Life could resume.

Being that I was living over an hour away at the time, I found it hard to get away from work to visit him. I called Mamaw periodically, and she assured me things were fine. *I'm just sitting here having a coke and a muffin for breakfast,* she said one day when she was on her way to the hospital. *Didn't have time for a real breakfast.* I could tell she was tired. I asked *Can I talk to Papaw? Or can you tell him I said hello and I'll be down to visit him soon?* I would have to confront the fear of going home and seeing my mother for the first time in nearly two years. Was I selfish for thinking of my own self-preservation? Would she even want to see me in the midst of all this mess? My stomach felt sick at the thought of going home. I had not been welcome at home for quite some time. The last time I went by the house when my parents weren't home (to visit my childhood dog), a questionable neighbor showed up with a gun saying that he kept watch and would notify people of any "unauthorized" visitor. I think I may have qualified as one of those people. I *know* Allison did.

*What, honey?* Mamaw continued. *I'm getting in the elevator and the phone is cutting out. Don't worry about us, dear. I'll tell Papaw you send your love.*

That was the last semblance of contact I had with my Papaw.

Days later, while he pedaled a bike during rehab, his heart stopped and never started again.

■ ■ ■

My mind rewound itself back to the present when I saw dad's name appear on my phone. It was a group message to me and my sister.

*I'm sorry girls. Papaw has died.*

I can't imagine how hard that was for my dad to type. At that very moment he was having to witness the implosion of my mother— I knew grief would strike her hard. Yet he took a moment to text us, not knowing the implications of what a death in the family might incite. Our family dynamics were hanging in the balance. I had to go home and face it all. Utter sorrow, fear, and anxiety overcame me.

"What happened?" Allison asked with a worried voice after I looked up from my phone.

I couldn't answer— instead, I curled up on the bed and wept.

This was a first for us. Neither of us had lost a family member in the course of our relationship, so this dance of pain and commiseration was a new one. What made it even harder was knowing that Allison's comfort couldn't follow me home. She had to remain an illusion. I wept for my grandfather, I wept for my mother, and I wept that I'd have to face it without the love of my life. After some scattered communication with family members, I found out the date of Papaw's funeral and began to muster emotional stamina in my heart. I played out worst-case scenarios in my mind and thought of civil responses (my therapist recommended, "I'm sorry you are hurting. I never intended to hurt you.") I was prepared for anything. Scenes from the movie *August: Osage County* flickered through my mind, too. I highly recommend the film to A) any Meryl Streep fans or B) anyone who loves a good, realistic, family systems nightmare of a movie. At risk of spoiling the plot line, the patriarch dies, and three daughters come home (I have two aunts) bringing with them emotional disparities that culminate in fiery monologues and the most heart wrenching cinematic drama I've ever seen. Throw in an angsty Julia Roberts and a mom who's addicted to pain pills, and it's a three-ring circus full of crisis. Granted my Mamaw isn't an addict, and I'm not secretly dating my cousin (spoiler alert), but some of the dynamics of the script hit *real* close to home.

Before I left for the funeral, Allison handed me a tiny seedling in a pot.

"Here, take this little plant to Mamaw," she said gently. Allison had been sprouting some flowers for out patio. I was happy to take a piece of her condolences along with me.

Before I left for home, I put on a little extra eye make-up and chose a less androgynous outfit. I didn't want to risk being ridiculed for "looking gay". My hair was already a target. I got in the car and began the long drive home, rehearsing the things I should say to civilly combat any negative comments. Anxiety had been manifesting in severe ways at that point in my life, and this circumstance was no exception. Shortness of breath and tightness in my chest nearly suffocated me as I fixated on the interstate. I listened to the rhythm of the horribly paved road and my panicked heartbeat as the miles-to-go ticked lower and lower. I pulled into my Mamaw's driveway, slightly relieved to find that she was one of the only ones at home. I stood at her door for five minutes, my hand hovering over the door knocker, wondering what I should say. Mamaw loved me and accepted me for who I was. I wasn't worried about ridicule from her— only worried that I couldn't find the right things to say, that I would have to see her cry, that it would hurt her more to have any further disarray caused by my coming home. All these things bombarded me, and I stood like a statue at the door until my aunt suddenly opened it.

"Here she is," my aunt said. She opened her arms and caught me in sweet hug. We hadn't spoken in a while.

Then I saw Mamaw get up from her chair and walk toward me. Terrified to utter something as meaningless as *I'm sorry for your loss*, I just hugged her and clutched the little plant so tightly in my hand that my knuckles turned white. We sat together in the den for a long while. Mamaw and Papaw had shared this fancy, dual recliner set-up with a connecting console. I watched her sit on her side occasionally gazing over to the empty chair beside her. My heart was broken. She proceeded to walk me through that hellish day, her panic, and her devastated realizations when the nurses ushered her into the chapel at the hospital instead of Papaw's room.

"I guess I really didn't fully understand 'til then," she said, shaking her head.

The afternoon drifted by, and I grew more and more anxious. I knew we were all gathering at my house for dinner, and I had yet to feel prepared for whatever this reunion held. I rode with my cousins and sat in the backseat of the car nervously picking at my fingernails. I pulled one into the quick. I winced. When we pulled into the driveway, I took a deep breath and got out of the car. My cousins, my sister, and I lingered in the yard making small talk about the shrubbery bed and other meaningless things. We were all deferring the inevitable, and I could tell that they all were carrying a little of my anxiety with them, too. When I stepped inside, the familiar smell of home hit me like a ton of bricks. My dad greeted me at the door and took my hand.

"Go talk to your mom," my dad said, slightly pulling me toward the kitchen.

"Come on now," Mamaw chimed in, "we're family." She was pushing me from behind.

"Everybody's just gonna have to get over it," my aunt agreed.

My head was swimming, and the pressure in my ears and head felt as if I were sinking into a deep pool. I remember being a kid and diving to the bottom of my grandparents' swimming pool to collect pennies we'd thrown in the deep end. A ten-foot dive was quite a feat for a ten year old, and I'd go in each time determined to gather more coins than my cousins. The chatter and sunlight grew dim at the bottom the pool. The pressure weighed down on my little frame, but I would scour the floor as long as I could in search of the pennies. Sometimes I'd stay down too long and my lungs would spasm, hungry for air.

I was pushed into the kitchen. I saw my mother hunched over the sink. The water was running, and she appeared to be washing dishes, but she was slumped over, sobbing. She lifted her head and looked at me for the first time in nearly two years. The pause was agonizing. I braced for manic yelling, demands to leave the house, ridicule for my short hair.

"My girl," she said through tears. She held me tight, sobbing apologies with every breath.

It was surreal. My Mamaw was crying out petitions and thanks to God. My dad hovered over us protectively as if some foreign force was threatening to pull us apart. My sister and family stood on the outskirts in tears. It was more of a spectacle than I had wanted. After what seemed like an hour, my mother let go. I imagined that everyone was about to break out into applause, but instead we all stood still. We waited. My mom rushed over to the cabinet and grabbed a plate. She went to the drawer and gathered some utensils. Seized by grief to a point of near disorientation, my mom moved erratically through the kitchen. She set a place at the head of the table, carefully positioning each piece.

"This place is for my daddy," she said adamantly.

It was a pitiful sight that left me reeling. What had just happened? The family started to move again, and everyone either headed for the dinner plates or the alcohol. The mood picked up, and people began laughing again. Gathered around the dinner table, we all made jokes and laughed until we cried. It started seeming like a holiday what with all the food and momentary disregard of our toxic differences. The rise-and-fall dichotomy of emotions in our family was a hallmark dynamic, and being back in the midst of it was exhausting but familiar (and oddly comforting). We continued eating, and for the first time in a long time, I was in community conversation with my mom. But I didn't know how to catch up. What could I talk about that wouldn't require an involved backstory or include Allison? I was suddenly distraught with realization—was everyone thinking that mine and mom's hug was complete reconciliation? Did everyone think I was brave and vulnerable enough to let them back in to the part of my life that had been the subject of so much mockery? Granted, the past election season had showcased everyone's malice-filled opinions, and it spewed out in such personal, attacking ways (on both sides, I will admit). It felt like children returning from preschool timeout, embarrassed and awkwardly staring at their fellow classmates. *Are we friends again? Do we forget this all happened, sit down, and play with these blocks again? The ones I just bashed across your head?* I was so scared that we would never be able to revisit that moment, that hug, and talk about it. It needed it to be analyzed, the ramifications assessed, a relationship trajectory charted. *Where do we go from here? Is this flicker of light one of hope?* Just as my mind was being bogged down in such details, I heard the dinner conversation turn towards the subject of tattoos.

"Yeah, Meredith, you should come with us!" one of my cousins called from across the table. "We are getting tattoos tonight in honor of Papaw."

"What? Really?" I stalled. I had more tattoos than anyone at that table, but I never got them impulsively, no matter what the circumstance. "Tell me more—I could be persuaded," I said.

"Well, we found some of his old letters and are going to get the artist to create a script piece that says *I love you too, sugar* in Papaw's own handwriting."

Whenever I called the house, Papaw always picked up the phone first. Without fail, on the second ring, Papaw answered with an iconic "MmmHello?" as if testing his voice a little before offering the salutation. His voice was precious. And recalling it made my eyes well with tears. Most times, I was calling to talk to Mamaw or to ask her a question, so mine and Papaw's conversation was often short-lived. I feel a twinge of guilt about that now. "I love you too, sugar. MmmBye-bye" he would say before handing the phone over to Mamaw. I will never forget the texture of his voice as he said those words. He said them to all of us. I couldn't refute the meaningfulness of a tattoo like that.

"We're going right now!" they all said in chorus. And they meant it, too.

Everyone suddenly got up from the table and started heading out to the car. A group our size was sure to give the tattoo parlor a shock. A total of seven people in my family were planning on getting the tattoo. As we began the drive, I grew a little nervous about how emotional (and not to mention intoxicated) my family was at the time. In circumstances like this, everyone was capable of either breaking out into tears or arguments. I picked at my fingernails again.

The artists at the parlor were very gracious and received us with a calm readiness. One by one, my family placed the purple template on their forearm, collar bone, or wrist, many of them going under the needle for the first time. I was still unsure about getting the tattoo, mainly because I have a newly-discovered heart condition that requires premedication before anything invasive. I sounded

like a prude saying it, but it was true. With only two artists working, the process was a long one. While I sat by as
moral support for my cousins, my mom suddenly grabbed
my hand.

"Let's go outside and talk," she said.

*Wonderful. This is what I've been waiting for—coming up with
a plan.*

"Sure thing," I said and readily followed.

I dodged the cigarette smoke of some patrons who
stood outside the parlor.

"I talked to my priest this week," she said, still holding tight to my hands, "and I asked him if we could cre-
mate Papaw with a [Catholic relic] even though he wasn't
Catholic." (I can not recall the exact word my mother
used here, and I don't want to misrepresent the holiness
of funeral rituals. Whatever the case, this piece was important to my mother). She continued, "My priest, he's from
India," she added. "He looked at me and said *Salvation is for
everyone.* I let that sink in, and it hit me for the first time:
why can't I apply that to my own daughter?"

I caught my breath and hoped she would continue in
this hopeful direction.

"So many times during the day, I encounter strangers
not knowing their background, their religion, or anything
about them. Yet I am kind to them, and I offer them love
like Christ would. Why can't I do that for my own daughter?" she asked again.

She was actually asking me *why*. It wasn't rhetorical.
She wanted to know why she was unable. I didn't know

what to say, so I continued doing the only thing I knew how to do in that moment—to simply listen. I wanted to meet her where she was and move on together. My therapist told me that the project of rebuilding would be one of the hardest things I would ever have to do. It would take both confidence in my true, individual self and rejection of all emotional responses. How would I respond to effectively affirm my mother after all this time?

"I love you more than I hate homosexuality," she said. "I don't want to be part of your relationship, but I want *you*."

My heart grimaced. Rather than the "two steps forward, one step back" analogy, I felt as if we were flitting around in circles—soaring toward something full of light only to fall back down into a dull place. Maybe we could swing up again into that cyclical and momentary hope.

"I still pray everyday that you'll change," she said and hugged me with a fervent desperation. "I hope you end up in heaven with me. Eternity is where we will understand this all, I guess. If you *aren't* there, at least heaven won't allow me to be sad about it. I love you, my girl."

I stood still, aching. "I love you too, Marmee."

I wanted to sob, yell, hold on forever, and run away at the same time. I wanted to mourn my grandfather, celebrate a breakthrough, and be anxious for what would happen next. Was this the resurrection of us? Were we seedlings fighting toward the sunlight, or were we both just dirt being flung on top of one another—stones from which unconditional understanding could never emerge?

These and many questions were left unanswered. Hand in hand, we buried a father and a grandfather. Side by side, we accompanied grief and confusion, finding common-ness in the hurt. *Give to the departed eternal rest. Let light per-petual shine upon them.*

I left home and headed *home*. Back to my soulmate, my best friend, the person I had asked to marry me. Allison and I were starting a life together, and for once, I was be-coming myself—praying that my mother would continue to grow somewhere alongside us. Chasing that perpetual light, I moved forward—believing in one God, maker of heaven and earth, of all that is, seen and unseen.

# APPENDIX
## A LETTER FROM BRANDI BURGESS

*"...I could tell you a thousand more stories, but mainly I just wanted to reach out. I would love to hear from you and correspond more. Your story has given me a little more hope- a little more courage to stay in the south and be the progressive voice it so needs."*

This was the closing paragraph to the message I received from Meredith, amidst hundreds, on January 13th, 2017. On the day I published my op-ed, "With Love from the Prodigal Daughter", I wasn't sure what to expect. I had been warned by al.com "not to read the comments", "prepare for backlash", "it may not be the reaction you're hoping for". I had been warned, begged, threatened not to publish. My father said "this is going to be ugly...

your brothers will be mocked and hurt by your desire to give yourself a platform...of all you could have done for the kingdom...I look forward to your repentance."

On January 13th, I heard my father's response to my article along with thousands of listeners. It was severe, heart-breaking, but not unexpected. I was braced for it. What I wasn't prepared for was Meredith, and the other children of parents that had received the same advice from my father, assuring that their child's salvation was null and void, that the only course of action was to doggedly pray for repentance and conversion. There were innumerable stories that so closely resembled mine. There were charitable organizations that lost his crucial funding for supporting LGBTQIA rights. There were former employees, shunned for sharing their heart's pursuit. There were hundreds of victims of his fear-mongering. I knew that hidden identities and subversive love were themes that ran strong in the South. I didn't realize that so many stories shared my father as a character.

I replied to all the messages I received. I read them over and over. They were the salve for my late night panic attacks, feelings of desolation, paralyzing grief and anger.

These beautiful individuals helped me feel God's light. I felt called to tell my story, felt it was important for my own freedom, but also perhaps for others like me. Meredith's voice joined the cacophony of others that whispered in the dark: "You are not alone, you are loved, you are wonderfully made".

In the days after my story went viral, all the doubts and fears creeped in. Was it wrong to tell my story? Was it selfish to go public, did I take the place of a more deserving story? My father wasn't changed, my family took his side, what was this all for?

Meredith then did something even more unprecedented. She went from being my ally to being a soldier of solidarity. She published an open letter to my father, sharing her story, refuting with grace and theological intelligence the biblical evidence he had railed against me.

Not only did her letter provide an evidence-based, rational approach to what God actually has been quoted on regarding love, but her choice to stand in the light with me, to endure the cruel comments with me, to compromise her private journey, all this served as a powerful reminder to why I did this, why I chose to come out.

Meredith brought me out of the darkness I was drowning in. Her piece, viewed over 12,000 times, spoke to me and countless others saying, "I am here, we are together, we must stand up and keep fighting. This all has a purpose, this isn't the end of your story, it is a chapter in our story".

As Southern queer folk, I believe it is time to come out of hiding. We must shine the light on oppression, cruelty, mis-cast prodigals. It can feel lonely, terrifying, narcissistic, even trite, but it is essential. We can no longer believe the lies that God's love is so narrow and discriminatory. It simply isn't true. We must fight fear with love, we must join our hands and chant into the night.

Meredith is my hero, I am honored to echo her cries into the sky, I am comforted by her honest expression of self-discovery, doubt, falling in love, self-loathing, empowerment, and peace.

My hand will forever be extended to her, and to you as well.

Let's carry on, let's live and love loudly.

Ever Yours,
Brandi

36090121R00135

Made in the USA
Middletown, DE
11 February 2019